The Encyclopedia of
Collectibles

TIME
LIFE ®
BOOKS

Other Publications:

The Epic of Flight

The Good Cook

The Seafarers

The Great Cities

World War II

Home Repair and Improvement

The World's Wild Places

The Time-Life Library of Boating

Human Behavior

The Art of Sewing

The Old West

The Emergence of Man

The American Wilderness

The Time-Life Encyclopedia of Gardening

Life Library of Photography

This Fabulous Century

Foods of the World

Time-Life Library of America

Time-Life Library of Art

Great Ages of Man

Life Science Library

The Life History of the United States

Time Reading Program

Life Nature Library

Life World Library

Family Library:
    How Things Work in Your Home
    The Time-Life Book of the Family Car
    The Time-Life Family Legal Guide
    The Time-Life Book of Family Finance

The Encyclopedia of
Collectibles

Radios to Signs

TIME-LIFE BOOKS, ALEXANDRIA, VIRGINIA

Time-Life Books Inc.
is a wholly owned subsidiary of
TIME INCORPORATED

Founder: Henry R. Luce 1898-1967

Editor-in-Chief: Henry Anatole Grunwald
President: J. Richard Munro
Chairman of the Board: Ralph P. Davidson
Executive Vice President: Clifford J. Grum
Editorial Director: Ralph Graves
Vice Chairman: Arthur Temple

TIME-LIFE BOOKS INC.
Managing Editor: Jerry Korn
Executive Editor: David Maness
Assistant Managing Editors: Dale M. Brown
(planning), George Constable,
Thomas H. Flaherty Jr. (acting), Martin Mann,
John Paul Porter
Art Director: Tom Suzuki
Chief of Research: David L. Harrison
Director of Photography: Robert G. Mason
Assistant Art Director: Arnold C. Holeywell
Assistant Chief of Research: Carolyn L. Sackett
Assistant Director of Photography: Dolores A. Littles

Chairman: Joan D. Manley
President: John D. McSweeney
Executive Vice Presidents: Carl G. Jaeger,
John Steven Maxwell, David J. Walsh
Vice Presidents: George Artandi (comptroller);
Stephen L. Bair (legal counsel); Peter G. Barnes;
Nicholas Benton (public relations);
John L. Canova; Beatrice T. Dobie (personnel);
Carol Flaumenhaft (consumer affairs);
James L. Mercer (Europe/South Pacific);
Herbert Sorkin (production); Paul R. Stewart
(marketing)

The Encyclopedia of Collectibles
Chief Researcher: Katie Hooper McGregor
Researcher: Ann Dusel Kuhns
Art Assistant: Mikio Togashi
Editorial Assistants: Jane Hanna, Dawn Patnode

Editorial Production
Production Editor: Douglas B. Graham
Operations Manager: Gennaro C. Esposito,
Gordon E. Buck (assistant)
Assistant Production Editor: Feliciano Madrid
Quality Control: Robert L. Young (director),
James J. Cox (assistant), Daniel J. McSweeney,
Michael G. Wight (associates)
Art Coordinator: Anne B. Landry
Copy Staff: Susan B. Galloway (chief),
Diane Ullius Jarrett, Brian Miller, Celia Beattie
Traffic: Jeanne Potter
Correspondents: Elisabeth Kraemer (Bonn); Margot
Hapgood, Dorothy Bacon, Lesley Coleman
(London); Susan Jonas, Lucy T. Voulgaris (New
York); Maria Vincenza Aloisi, Josephine du Brusle
(Paris); Ann Natanson (Rome). Valuable assistance
was also provided by: Karin B. Pearce (London);
Carolyn T. Chubet, Miriam Hsia, Christina
Lieberman (New York); Mimi Murphy (Rome).

The Encyclopedia of Collectibles
was created under the supervision
of Time-Life Books by
TREE COMMUNICATIONS, INC.
President: Rodney Friedman
Publisher: Bruce Michel
Vice President: Ronald Gross
Secretary: Paul Levin

For information about any Time-Life book, please write:
Reader Information
Time-Life Books
541 North Fairbanks Court
Chicago, Illinois 60611
Library of Congress Cataloguing in Publication Data
Main entry under title:
    The encyclopedia of collectibles.
    Includes bibliographies.
    1. Americana. 2. Antiques—United States.
I. Time-Life Books.
NK805.E63   745.1'09'0973   77-99201
ISBN 0-8094-2764-8
ISBN 0-8094-2763-X lib. bdg.

© 1980 Time-Life Books Inc. All rights reserved.
No part of this book may be reproduced in any form or by
any electronic or mechanical means, including information
storage and retrieval devices or sytems, without prior
written permission from the publisher, except that brief
passages may be quoted for reviews.
Second printing.
Published simultaneously in Canada.
School and library distribution by Silver Burdett Company,
Morristown, New Jersey.

TIME-LIFE is a trademark of Time Incorporated U.S.A.

Printed in U.S.A.

The Encyclopedia of Collectibles
Editor: Andrea DiNoto
Art Director: Sara Burris
Director of Research: Heidi Sanford
Research Coordinator: Cathy Cashion
Photographers: David Arky, Steven Mays
Assistant Art Director: Christopher Jones
Art Assistant: David Nehila
Researchers: Sally Clark, Howard Cohn,
Gretchen Dykstra, Carole Ann Fabian,
Deborah Gale, Carol Gaskin, Amy Gateff,
Scott Hudson, Jannika Hurwitt, Janis Kaye,
Don Kennedy, Bill Logan, Margaret Mooney,
Jay Stevens, Russell Stockman, Leslie Teicholz,
Ann Yarowsky, Susan Wasserstein
Writers: Bruce Chadwick, Colin Leinster,
Barbara Leish, Judson Mead, Fred Poole,
Ellen Posner, David Schraffenberger,
Marguerite Tarrant, Henry Wiencek
Editorial Assistant: Kathleen Hushion

Editorial Consultant: Jay Gold
Consultants for this volume: Rod Phillips (Radios);
Howie Samelson (Railroadiana); Susan H. Myers
(Redware); Adam White (Rock and Roll
Memorabilia); George C. Humphrey (Rogers
Groups); David Newsam (Royal Souvenirs); Glee
Krueger (Samplers); Elton Hall (Scrimshaw); Peter
Laskovski, June Sprigg (Shaker Crafts); Rick Lee
(Signs)

Acknowledgments: Atwater Kent radio, page 11, Sears
Silvertone, page 14, Zenith radio, bottom, page 15, all
radios, pages 16, 17, Waves, Inc., New York City; menu,
page 29, Louis Szathmary, Chicago, Illinois; Grizzly Flats
Railroad, pages 30, 31, Ward Kimball, San Gabriel,
California; Indian pottery, pages 42, 43, courtesy Museum
of the American Indian, Heye Foundation, New York City;
button, page 50, hat, page 55, sneakers, button, dolls, page
58, wig, page 59, Speakeasy Antiques, New York City;
poster, page 51, Michael King, Andover, Massachusetts;
Everly Brothers record, page 56, all records, page 57,
Beatles record, page 59, Dave Clark Five record, Beach
Boys record, page 61, House of Oldies, 267 Bleecker
Street, New York City; poster, page 62, Jack Rennert, New
York City; Hummels, pages 68, 69, Robert Mascarelli,
Bellmore, New York; coronation coach, pages 84, 85, Dr.
Hilton Read, Ventnor City, New Jersey; sampler, page 89,
sampler, top right, page 92, map sampler, page 93,
sampler, page 96, sampler, page 99, Mr. and Mrs. David
Kemp, Windsor Antiques, Scarsdale, New York; sampler,
page 90, Glee Krueger, Westport, Connecticut; sampler,
pages 94, 95, Mary Lou Sutter, White Plains, New York;
mottoes at bottom, page 98, Kelter-Malcé Antiques, New
York City; motto at top, page 98, Ethel's Feathers, New
York City; all items, pages 110, 111, Jerry Ohlinger, Movie
Material Store, New York City; postcard, page 125,
Andreas Brown, Gotham Book Mart, New York City;
spinning wheel, page 128, collection of Hancock Shaker
Village, Pittsfield, Massachusetts, photographed by Paul
Rocheleau, reproduced by permission of *The Magazine
Antiques*; mug at top, scuttle mug, page 142, mug, page
143, three razors at top, page 144, Warren Moore, Ramsey,
New Jersey; razor at top, page 145, reprinted with
permission of the Gillette Company; razor at bottom, page
144, razor at bottom, page 145, courtesy of A. R. Booth,
Personal Products Division, Warner-Lambert Company
(manufacturer of Schick razor blades); signs, page 158, sign
at top, page 159, Robert English, Marshfield Hills,
Massachusetts; rubbing, page 159, Cecily Barth Firestein,
New York City; sign, page 160, Al Higger, New York City.

The Cover: Rare occupational shaving mugs show, from
the left: (top row) a waiter, a boilermaker, an airplane pilot;
(middle row) firemen, a teacher, a machine operator;
(bottom row) a steam-shovel operator, a billposter and a
diner operator. The last mug and the pilot's are two and
three times as valuable as any of the others.

Contents

Radios
Tuning In to Yesteryear

Radios captured my imagination early. Like many boys of the time, I built a set of my own in 1927, when I was eight years old. Since then I have put together at least 1,000. Nevertheless, I knew little about radio history when I set out to become a collector. I simply started driving around to neighboring towns and knocking on the doors of older homes. I found some early radios at good prices in just this way—and I stumbled onto a real bonanza just about two months after I started collecting.

A man offered me a bushel basket full of old parts for $50; I was bargaining with him on his front lawn when

---

Ralph Muchow, a dentist in Elgin, Illinois, began his collection of nearly 2,000 sets in 1967. He has restored them all to working order.

---

rain began to fall. Afraid that the rain would ruin the parts, I quickly raised my offer and closed the deal. After I got the parts home I discovered that they were the components of an Atwater Kent model 5—an AK5 to a collector—one of the most desired of antique radios. Not many were made—the AK5 did not work very well—and only 13 are known to survive.

The AK5 appeared in 1923, when radio had yet to become an intimate part of daily life, although communication by wireless had been established for several decades. Inventor Guglielmo Marconi had demonstrated its practicability in the 1890s. In 1901 the American Marconi Wireless Telegraph Company began handling messages transmitted in dot-dash telegraph code, and the armed forces of most countries soon bought similar equipment for their signal services. Examples of the wireless apparatus used in the early 1900s are very desirable to collectors; they are difficult to find and many are hard to identify because they resemble the telegraph equipment of the time.

The radios most collectors find are not commercial or military communications devices but the home sets built after the development of the vacuum tube, which made possible transmission of voices and music. At first most sets were home-built and in many cases home-designed. Some amateurs built transmitters and receivers so that they could communicate with one another. Many more people built receivers so that they could eavesdrop on

the airwave chatter. Such sets, made before 1920, are very rare and desirable.

The majority of collectible radios date from the beginning of commercial broadcasting, on November 2, 1920, when station KDKA went on the air in Pittsburgh with news of President Warren Harding's election. The radio receiver became a home appliance you could buy—although many were homemade—and collectors seek the landmark models that are significant for appearance, popularity or technical innovation. Three main types are recognized: the early sets that could be listened to only with earphones; the battery-powered loudspeaker models that were popular until 1927; and the succeeding loudspeaker models that operated from regular house current. Radios from the 1920s and early 1930s are the most desirable, although there also is interest in models of the later 1930s. The cutoff date for collecting is generally the invention of the transistor—1947—which changed radios into the form they have today.

Radio broadcasting had to overcome a great deal of skepticism—"I don't hold with furniture that talks," grumped one comedian. Public acceptance was hampered by primitive receiving equipment. To listen to early broadcasts, people had to don headphones and fiddle with the cat's whisker of a crystal set *(page 8)*. The whisker was a movable wire of copper, brass or silver with which the would-be listener poked at a piece of lead sulfide to tune in a signal picked up by a long antenna strung outside the house. At best, such a set could bring in one or two nearby stations, scratchy with static, and then only after considerable probing with the cat's whisker to find the "sensitive" spot on the crystal. Old crystal sets are hard to find now and correspondingly valuable, although in the early 1920s they were cheap and plentiful, many of them made at home from inexpensive kits.

After 1921, radios with loudspeakers enabled the whole family to listen, a change made possible by the introduction of receivers with circuits that contained vacuum-tube amplifiers. Tuning was still something of a

The 1931 Philco Superheterodyne 90B is an early example of the so-called cathedral sets, table models that became popular during the Depression. Today they are fairly easy to find, but collectors prize them for the old-fashioned charm of their design.

Crystal sets like this 1924 Beaver Baby Grand are now rare and valued far above their original cost, around $10. The tuning mechanism con- *sists mainly of a piece of crystalline lead sulfide (in the cylinder at rear) and the fine wire called the cat's whisker touching the crystal.*

feat: All sets of this period can be recognized by the multiplicity of dials on their front panels, which somewhat resemble the many knobs on today's costly stereo sets.

A dedicated listener trying to tune the Leutz Super-Heterodyne model L of 1923 had to work 27 dials and knobs to bring in the station he wanted. Two desirable examples of multitube, multidial sets are the CR9 made by A. H. Grebe & Co. and the model V made by the Colin B. Kennedy Company. Both of these had improved circuitry that allowed them to bring in stations that were farther away and to separate their signals more effectively for listening ease.

By the early 1920s, engineers had figured out how to gang the components of the tuning circuits so that one knob changed all components simultaneously, and tuning became the simple one-dial operation it is today. The Atwater Kent AK5 is an early example of one-dial tuning. Another now sought by collectors is the TRF5 made in 1924 by the Magnavox Company.

Although radios from the mid-1920s had loudspeakers and eventually became easy to use, they still required

cumbersome wet batteries like those in cars. The batteries dripped acid on the rug and had to be lugged off periodically for recharging. This nuisance was ended in 1927 when a way was found to operate the vacuum tubes from an ordinary electrical outlet without introducing an audible low hum from the 60-times-a-second alternation of house current. Sales soared. The leading manufacturer was now the RCA Company, which was also important in phonographs and a giant in broadcasting, with two national networks. The most popular plug-in set was RCA's Electrola Radiola. In addition to the Radiola, collectors also look for the more expensive Stromberg-Carlsons (models 744B, 14B and 654B) and Zeniths (models 40A, 55 and 67). These are desired as much for their fine cabinetry as for the fact that they had better reception than many competing sets.

By the 1930s such receivers enabled weekly family gatherings to laugh at and with Will Rogers, Jack Benny, Fred Allen and Eddie Cantor. And powerful public figures were beginning to discover that the effective use of radio could alter the course of events. Two sets popular

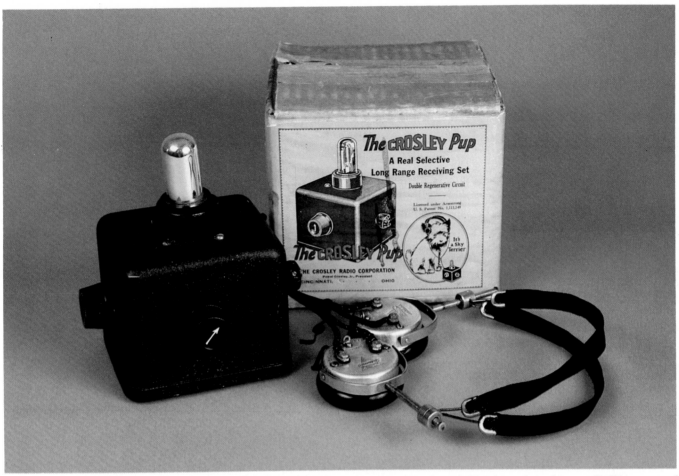

A simple vacuum tube in the 1925 Crosley Pup above did the work of the cat's whisker and crystal used in crystal sets (left). The Pup, one of the first inexpensive but reliable tube receivers, is easy to find. It was one of the few single-tube sets to attach the tube to the top of the cabinet.

at that time—partly because they were affordable during the Depression—were the Philco 90B, one of the first plug-in table radios, and the General Electric Highboy, a full-sized set of good quality at a low price. As political storm clouds gathered in Europe and led into World War II, the nation kept up with the news by listening to such radios as the Silvertones *(page 14)*, sold by Sears, Roebuck & Company, and the Magnavox Heppelwhite, which offered an advanced speaker system.

After World War II, two revolutions changed the nature of radio. The first, of course, was the advent of television, which quickly captured the prime-time evening audience and forced radio into new programing patterns. The second revolution was the invention of the transistor, which signaled a new era in radio technology and the end, for many, of radio's collectible period.

Finding radios from the 1920s and 1930s is not a great problem. Many examples still are available at flea markets and garage sales. The most valuable are those that contain all their original parts in working order. However, most will not work. Some people settle hap-

pily for what is called a static display—all the tubes are in the right sockets, and condensers, resistors, transformers, chokes and binding posts are in place, but the radios do not play. Such a display is only tantalizing to devoted collectors; they want old radios that play.

Troubleshooting and repairing old radios is, in these transistorized days, a nearly lost art, and modern repairmen are unlikely to help you restore most models. Worse, replacement parts and basic repair information—wiring diagrams and service data, for instance—may not be available.

However, many sets had wiring diagrams pasted inside the cabinets, and service guidance can sometimes be found in books *(page 19)* or by asking in a large public library for back issues of radio publications such as *Radio News* and *Popular Radio*. To establish the date an old set was made—and thus narrow the search for service information—try to match it against pictures in old advertisements in such popular magazines of the 1920s and 1930s as *Collier's* and *The Saturday Evening Post,* back issues of which are available in many libraries. Some manufacturers—notably RCA and Zenith—can provide technical information on their old sets.

Some of the old types of tubes, condensers and coils still may be available from electronics-supply houses, listed in the classified telephone book. But most such parts no longer are stocked. Collectors scavenge for them, buying inoperable radios to disassemble for good parts and trading with fellow collectors. Offers of swaps also appear in the newsletters published by some of the collectors' organizations *(page 19)*.

Many collectors make the playability problem more manageable by limiting themselves to collecting just one type of radio, such as crystal sets, which are very small, are easy to work and need no batteries; or such simple tube receivers from the mid-1920s as the Crosley Pup *(page 9)*. But the purists will not go so far as to make an old radio appear playable by replacing its innards with a transistor radio.

As for the question of price, I believe that most collectors are fair with one another, but you must remember that values are relative; ultimately a radio is worth what a buyer is willing to pay for it. A collector who needs a model 5 to complete his collection of Atwater Kents will pay more than a person who already owns one. And with the mass-produced radios of the 1940s, values can

shift abruptly. A model might be scarce one day, but 50 more like it could turn up in a warehouse tomorrow.

While the internal condition of an old set is a major determinant of value, external condition also is important. A few scratches on the cabinet are to be expected, but if the front panel is mashed, if dials and knobs are missing, the receiver is probably worth no more than the value of its components as replacement parts. Collectible value is also influenced by the original selling price; for example, sets made by Atwater Kent and Stromberg-Carlson were expensive when new and remain so today.

If you have the space, some of the best buys are the grand consoles—radios intended to serve as impressive pieces of furniture. Among the more desirable are Philco models 116 and 200X, the Magnavox Berkeley and Regent, Zenith models 245 and 441 and, above all, Scott Radio Laboratories' Imperial, All-Wave Deluxe and Philharmonic. All but the last of these consoles are ranked approximately equal in value by collectors; the Scott Philharmonic commands a premium.

Scotts were to the '30s what Atwater Kents were to the '20s; to me they are the finest of vintage radios. Founder E. H. Scott thought so too, and he was not shy about saying so. His advertising slogan was "If you can tolerate any other radio, please don't buy a Scott."

High style and high technology meet in this 1926 Splitdorf battery-powered radio, sought by collectors because it is among the first to be made with only one tuning dial. The speaker is inside the fancifully painted conch shell.

Collectors value all Atwater Kent sets as radios of excellent quality. The 1924 model 10C shown above is one of the breadboard series, so called because the components were set out on an open board, easily accessible, rather than being enclosed in a cabinet.

Microphones of the early 1920s like these two, adapted from telephone equipment, proved unreliable. They were filled with carbon granules that tended to pack, and the mike sometimes had to be struck in mid-broadcast to loosen them. Early carbon microphones are valued but fairly common.

Condenser microphones like the one at right replaced the carbon type. Collectors seek this square version because such stars as Jack Benny were photographed with one.

The Frightening Microphone

Some collectors of radios prize early microphones not only because they were essential elements in the broadcasting process but also because they take up little space in a collection. The microphone posed a problem for early broadcasters, especially those producing dramas over the air. Actors suffered so acutely from what was dubbed mike fright that ingenious tricks were employed to disguise their presence. The WGY Players of Schenectady, New York, for instance, put lamp shades over their microphone stands, hoping that what the actors did not see they would not fear.

Early microphones also caused problems for engineers. At first, broadcasters simply adapted telephone mouthpieces, but these proved inadequate. They were superseded by the more sensitive condenser microphone *(above, right).* This instrument reacts to sound waves with delicate variations in a stored electrical force, not to changes in electrical resistance as telephone devices do.

The 1927 model 36, a console set, was the first Atwater Kent that could be operated from regular house current, and is valued by collectors for that reason. Finely made cabinets and the absence of batteries made such console radios handsome additions to living-room furniture.

This easy-to-find Sears Silvertone, one of the first radios having more than one reception band, received police, short-wave and regular broadcasts.

The 1931 Crosley Wigit is much sought after because it is an early, small cathedral set, so called because the cabinet shape vaguely resembles an ornate Gothic arch.

This 1934 Zenith model 835 has the same circuitry as the Silvertone console shown opposite. Originally the console cost more, but today's collectors, who are often short of space, would value the two models about equally.

Small molded-plastic radios like these '40s and '50s models are common. The two in front were made by the F. A. D. Andrea Corporation; the one at left can receive

short-wave broadcasts. At left rear is an RCA that also receives short waves next to a Crosley portable that can operate on dry-cell batteries or household current.

The 1930s and 1940s spawned a profusion of colorful novelty sets. This 1935 Smokerette, made by Porto-Products, combines a radio with a pipe rack, a humidor, a cigarette box and an ashtray. Originally priced at $50, the Smokerette is a valuable find for a collector.

Radios adorned with depictions of popular personalities, real or fictional, were among the widely sold novelty sets. Ventriloquist's dummy Charlie McCarthy is on the Majestic radio at left. The Dionne quintuplets adorn the Stewart Warner set. Both of these are very desirable.

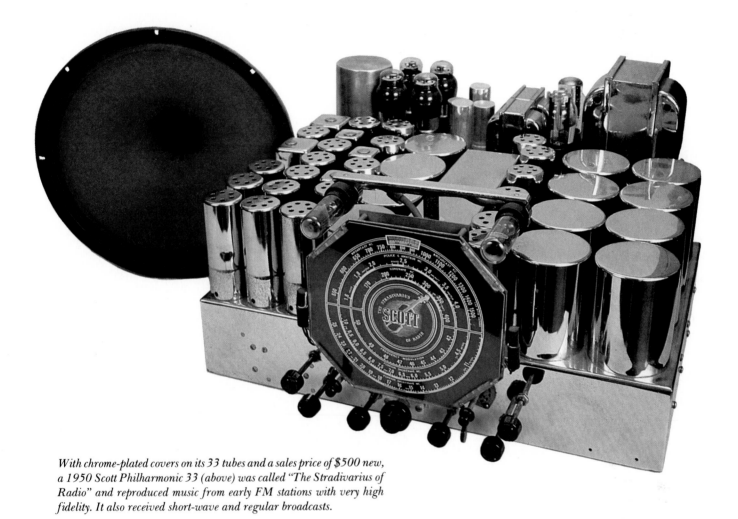

With chrome-plated covers on its 33 tubes and a sales price of $500 new, a 1950 Scott Philharmonic 33 (above) was called "The Stradivarius of Radio" and reproduced music from early FM stations with very high fidelity. It also received short-wave and regular broadcasts.

MUSEUMS
National Broadcaster's Hall of Fame
Freehold, New Jersey 07728

Smithsonian Institution
Museum of History and Technology
Washington, D.C. 20560

COLLECTORS ORGANIZATIONS
Antique Radio Club of America
81 Steeplechase Road
Devon, Pennsylvania 19333

Antique Wireless Association
4 Main Street
Holcomb, New York 14469

BOOKS
Barnouw, Erik, *A History of Broadcasting in the United States.* 2 vols. Oxford University Press, 1966, 1968.

Beitman, Morris N., *Most-Often-Needed 1926-1938 Radio Diagrams* (facsimile). Vintage Radio, Box 1331, North Highlands, California 95660, originally published 1941.

Dreher, Carl, *Sarnoff: An American Success.* New York Times Book Company, 1977.

Gernsback, Sidney, *S. Gernsback's Radio Encyclopedia.* Vintage Radio, 1974.

Lessing, Lawrence, *Man of High Fidelity: Edwin Howard Armstrong.* J. P. Lippincott Company, 1956.

McMahon, Morgan:
A Flick of the Switch, 1930-1950. Vintage Radio, 1975.
Radio Collector's Guide. Vintage Radio, 1975.
Vintage Radio. Vintage Radio, 1973.

Puett, J. W. F., *Silver Ghosts.* Puett Electronics, P.O. Box 28572, Dallas, Texas 75228, 1975.

Railroadiana
Remembering the Iron Horse

Fading from most Americans' memories are the pleasures that the railroads once brought—the reassuring musical note of the steam locomotive's whistle in the night, the treat of a lavish meal in the dining car, the exhilaration of speeding smoothly through towns and fields. The steam locomotive is gone from all but lines operated solely for amusement. And the train was long ago eclipsed as long-distance transportation by the automobile and the airplane.

But following the tracks of the great trains of yesterday—the Twentieth Century Limited, Zephyr, Orange Blossom Special, Oriental Limited, Super Chief, City of

---

Dave Peters Sr., who worked for railroads in New England for 18 years, first felt the lure of the rails as he stared out the school window at trains when he was in the fifth grade.

Portland, Wabash Cannonball—are thousands of ardent collectors. They cherish an amazing variety of railroadiana that recaptures the days of the iron horse.

All collectors prize artifacts from the age of the steam-powered locomotive, which came to an end in the 1950s. But items associated with the diesel and electric era that followed are more available, and many collectors concentrate on them. Subways, trolleys, cable cars and interurbans—intercity trolleys—also have their loyal collectors. Thousands of such lines have operated in the United States, and each put its name or initials on just about everything its employees used in the course of their work. A key with the letters *NYC* once opened a switch lock on the New York Central. A lantern marked *SP* once signaled an engineer on the Southern Pacific Railroad. Collectors may specialize in a particular line, and to them its name and initials are magical. Some seek items from plush dining and sleeping cars with such evocative names as Winter Park, Marcia, Stag Hound and Flying Fish.

Because objects from older lines are more valuable— a ticket bearing the name of the New York Central or the Pennsylvania Railroad is more desirable than one made after those lines merged to form the Penn Central—a knowledge of railroad history is almost essential, and experienced collectors become walking repositories of arcane data. In the scheme of collecting values, an item from an obscure railroad, one that ran for just a short distance for a short time, is almost always more valuable than something similar from a larger, longer-lived railroad.

Some of the scarcest examples come from late-19th Century lines such as the Carson & Colorado, which ran from Nevada to neighboring Colorado; the Eureka & Palisade in Nevada; the York & Peachbottom of Pennsylvania; the Bridgton & Saco River of Maine; and the Deland & St. Johns in Florida. Colorado in particular had many narrow-gauge railroads, whose rails were laid closer together than the standard gauge of four feet 8½ inches. Among these were the Denver, South Park & Pacific and the Florence & Cripple Creek; like many Colorado narrow-gauge lines, they were built to haul ore and miners, and went out of business when the mines were exhausted.

For every railroad there are two types of collectibles—paper and hardware. The most commonly collected of paper items is the timetable, widely available and therefore of modest value. The oldest timetables are simple—a single sheet printed on one side. They had become more elaborate by the turn of the century, with lithographed illustrations of luxurious dining cars and powerful locomotives. These early timetables often have interesting footnotes and revealing advisories. One from the 1880s refused to promise exactly when passengers would reach their destination. It simply stated, "Passengers will be conveyed as quickly as possible to the end of the line."

Before nationwide standard time came into being in 1883—it was a measure sponsored by the railroads— the lines had to cope with local time. Cities set their own clocks by the sun. An 1877 Pennsylvania timetable advised passengers, "Standard Time of the Pennsylvania Railroad . . . from New York to Pittsburgh is Philadelphia local time, which is five minutes slower than New

In the basement of his home, author Dave Peters has re-created a railroad ticket office. The window grille and tabletop came from the Wallingford, Connecticut, train station of the New York, New Haven and Hartford Railroad. Below the 1897 calendar at upper left are tickets. The rubber stamps and ticket punches were used over a period of more than half a century, from 1890 to 1950.

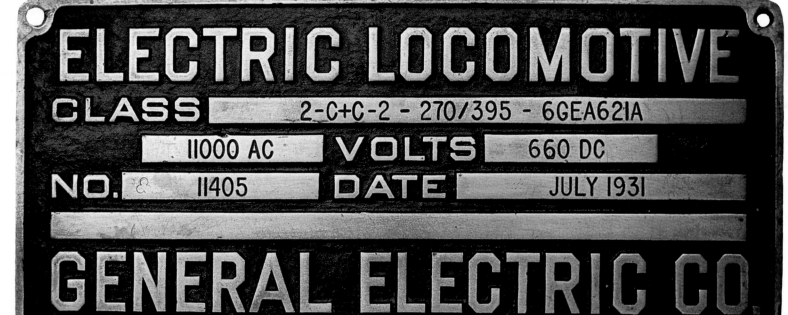

ELECTRIC LOCOMOTIVE
CLASS 2-C+C-2 - 270/395 - 6GEA621A
11000 AC VOLTS 660 DC
NO. 8 11405 DATE JULY 1931
GENERAL ELECTRIC CO.
SCHENECTADY, N.Y., U.S.A.

Every locomotive carried a builder's plate indicating place and date of manufacture and, for some locomotives, technical specifications. The example above identified an electric model used by the New Haven line in the 1930s. Plates are scarce and highly desirable.

York time and 19 minutes faster than Pittsburgh time."

For the use of conductors and crew, the railroads printed employee timetables, which generally are hard to find and highly desirable. They are also of special interest to collectors because of the technical information they provide—speed limits, the weight capacities and heights of bridges, and the locations of repair facilities. Desirable for similar reasons are trainmen's rule books, which offer fascinating glimpses of passenger-employee relations. The Erie Railroad's 1908 "Rules of the Operating Department" informed conductors that the laws regarding passengers who did not pay their fares differed from state to state. In Illinois, "a passenger and his baggage may be ejected without unnecessary force. This statute does not state where, but he should not be put off on a bridge or other dangerous place; on the contrary, a safe and proper place should be selected."

Other paper items sought by collectors include matchbooks, calendars, trade cards, postcards and posters. Many lines sold playing cards on trains for the entertainment of passengers—and occasionally to the profit of professional gamblers. One collector has a sign that reads, "Warning: The Pullman Company calls the attention of its patrons to the fact that 'Card Sharks' and 'Con Men' have started their winter campaign on railroad trains. Passengers can protect themselves by refusing to play with strangers."

Few paper collectibles are as valuable as what collectors loosely refer to as hardware. The category is enormous, including uniforms, lanterns, locks and keys, nails, ticket punches, tableware, bells, locomotive headlights and, ultimately, whole cars and locomotives. One collector, a retired mailman in Connecticut, has six Pullman cars in his three-acre backyard, for which he paid $1,000 each in the early 1960s. Ward Kimball of California not only collected a railroad for his backyard but operates it there *(pages 30-31)*.

Uniforms are widely collected, and they are fairly easy to find because many trainmen saved their uniforms. Caps are a particular favorite. Aficionados turn up at gatherings of collectors sporting hats labeled "Ticket Agent," "Brakeman" or "Baggage Handler."

Other objects form specialized collections. A whole class of collectors has sprung up around dining-car items. Most lines had their own china design, and complete table settings are prized. Ashtray collecting is an old, if not always honorable, avocation. The railroads assumed that riders would pocket ashtrays decorated with the line's logotype, and considered the loss a form of advertising. Similarly, the railroads put their names

This foot-high brass whistle, made around 1870, can sound three notes—but only if powered by compressed air at a pressure of 110 pounds per square inch.

The bell above, cast around 1920, bears marks not visible in the picture to indicate it once rang on locomotive 0107 on the New Haven line. The collector acquired it at a scrapyard in 1971.

and logos on linen—napkins, towels, blankets and head-rest covers that were filched then and are collected now.

Harder to come by are the technical devices the public rarely saw, such as locks and keys. Some collectors of keys, oddly enough, have no interest in locks. Locks were produced in a number of shapes for switches, tool-boxes and equipment sheds. The most valuable of all are brass locks in the shape of a heart, which were made before World War II. Nails are another item of collect-ible small railroad hardware—if they are date nails, which were used to mark new railroad ties with the date of installation and thus provide a check on their usable life *(page 25)*.

Date nails are one item a collector can find by simply walking along an old track—if many collectors have not walked there before him. Many items of railroadiana are found at flea markets, estate sales, and antique and junk shops—as well as in the attics of railroad men who have gone to ride with Casey Jones, the Wabash Cannonball engineer who was immortalized in song for his heroic death in a 1900 crash.

Railroads themselves are a fertile source of collect-ibles. When newspapers report that part of a line is go-ing out of business, I make a call to the supply depart-ment of the company to ask if anything is for sale. I once

paid a visit to the sign painter's shop in New York City's Grand Central Station, where I was able to get a dozen old roll signs, which displayed all of the stops that a train would make, in exchange for a tin of the painter's favorite tobacco.

My greatest collecting coup involved an 1880 conduc-tor's lantern. Lanterns usually consist of three main parts in metal—base, chimney and wire guard—plus a glass globe. Because the globe was likely to be broken, lanterns are seldom found intact today. I was rummag-ing around the attic of an old station in Connecticut when I found the chimney of a lantern from the New Haven Railroad. I showed it to a fellow collector, who said he had a base that was made for that kind of lan-tern. I put the two pieces together and found that they fit. About a year and a half later I bought a glass globe that is engraved with a floral pattern and a conductor's name, C. F. Bassett. I got it at an auction for a few dol-lars. At home I tried attaching it to several old lanterns without success, until I slipped it into the New Haven lantern—a perfect fit. That authentically restored lan-tern *(page 27)*, with its one-of-a-kind globe, might now be worth a tidy sum but I will never part with it. It swung in the night 100 years ago, signaling the engineer of a train that has long since steamed into history.

Models from the Patent Office

Scale models of old railroad hardware—including switches, lanterns, frame-and-wheel assemblies called trucks, and even entire cars—sometimes can be found in the form of patent models, required with every patent application until 1880. The period coincided with the years when railroad technology was being developed most rapidly, and many patents related to railroads. However, only one model was required for each invention, and surviving models are scarce. Most show the name of the inventor, the function and the patent number.

The patent model at left, 10 inches long, is for a one-man handcar propelled by a crank and gears. The model was submitted to the United States patent office in 1860.

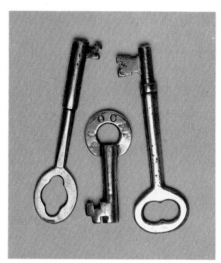

Locks and keys are easily found. The two long keys above opened coaches around 1910; the short 1890 key worked switch locks on the Old Colony line in Massachusetts.

At right are an 1890s New Haven freight-car door lock (upper left), a 1920s New York, Westchester & Boston signal lock (top right), and a 1950s Central Vermont switch lock.

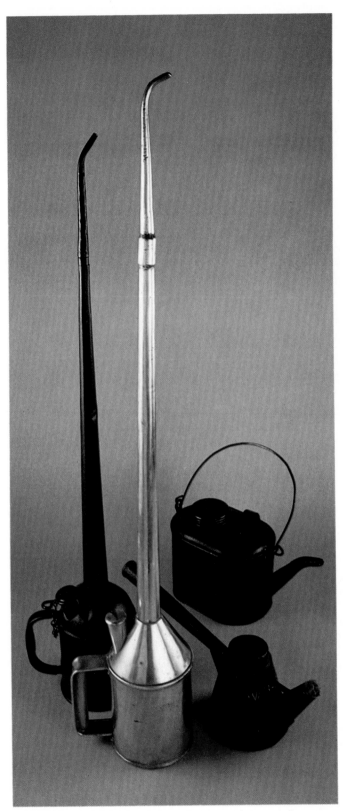

The collector found this rare cast-iron switch stand with its signal lamp near a depot in Berlin, Connecticut. It dates from the early 1900s. The colors of the lights indicated the direction in which the switch was set.

A tin kerosene torch (lower right) and three oilcans, used on steam locomotives in the 1930s and 1940s, are desirable hardware items. The one at upper right was for oiling valves; at left is a typical all-purpose oiler. Next to it is a rare brass oilcan, a presentation for years of service.

Nails with numbers on their heads are date nails, pounded into ties to record the year each was put in place. The numbers show the last two digits of a year; thus the nails shown were used between 1912 and 1931. Discontinued by most railroads in the 1940s, date nails are easy to find.

Virtually any part of a railroader's uniform is collectible, but hats are especially favored. The one above carries the *badge of a conductor on the New Haven line and stars (one is visible at the left) for every 10 years of service.*

The three plates above, badges that were affixed to the hats of on-train employees, identify their duties. Badges like the ones that are pictured frequently turn up at flea markets.

Thrifty wives often saved cuff, vest and coat buttons when uniforms wore out. The conductor's button from the Boston & Maine Railroad — one of the nation's oldest lines — is from the turn of the century.

Ticket punches made identifiable holes. The one at top punches out BC for "baggage checked," the example at bottom punches 1 and 2 to denote half-fare tickets, and the one at center is a cancellation symbol.

This 19th Century conductor's lantern, its owner's name engraved on the glass globe, is the collector's prized possession. Its long bail permits it to be swung in a wide arc to signal the engineer.

Official railroad watches — the railroad man's classic accouterment — are much sought after. This 1940 model has a lever over the 1 that locks the hands so they cannot be reset inadvertently while the spring is wound.

This chair, the acme in parlor-car comfort in 1940, was made for the Pennsylvania Railroad. It has aluminum sides; Tuscan-red fabric; and a headrest cover showing an electric locomotive, the U.S. Capitol dome and the Washington Monument. The chair swivels and reclines.

Plates like this, part of an eight-piece place setting made for the Baltimore & Ohio Railroad, are popular for their depictions of that line's famous locomotives.

Menus are easily found and widely collected. Many are attractively printed, and the low prices they list cause twinges of nostalgia. The 19th Century menu above depicts the interior of a dining car named Grande Australia.

Plush Pullman dining cars boasted a variety of silverware bearing the company's name, including this caster, which sprinkled cinnamon and sugar for the traveler's morning toast.

The elegant china at left, bearing the logotype of a line that ran from Buffalo to Chicago and St. Louis until after World War II, was made in limited quantity and is hard to find.

Ward Kimball (in background above) presides over the Grizzly Flats depot, complete with railroad prints and 1890 potbellied stove.

One Man's Railroad

The ultimate railroad collectible is a backyard railroad, a fantasy that only a few collectors in the world have realized. One such collector is Ward Kimball of San Gabriel, California—who with his wife, Betty, runs the 900-foot-long Grizzly Flats Railroad, named for a California mining town that now is a posh retirement resort.

Kimball started building his railroad in 1938 at the age of 24, when he purchased for $400 a steam locomotive on its way to a Japanese scrapyard. Since then he has acquired another locomotive, a caboose, four other cars, a windmill to pump water into a storage tank, and hundreds of other railroad collectibles, which he houses in a depot *(above)* modeled on an 1855 depot of the Pottsville branch of the Lehigh Valley line. In 1949 one fantasy merged with another when the Walt Disney studio, where Kimball worked for many years as an animator (he created the character Jiminy Cricket), gave him the depot, which had first been used as a set for the film *So Dear to My Heart.*

The Emma Nevada (left), a coal burner weighing 22 tons from the Nevada Central Railroad, builds up steam for its run of 900 feet.

Annual passes were handed out to politicians, favored businessmen and railroad employees. The three pictured above are from the turn of the century.

Timetables are collected for their colorful illustrations and the wealth of information they provide about lines that are now gone. Most are fairly easy to find.

Many railroads used postcards as a form of advertising and promotion. The Pennsylvania Railroad issued this card in 1939, showing the spectacular 180-degree turn of Horse Shoe Curve outside Altoona, Pennsylvania.

Railroad stock certificates, most of which display a standard likeness of a locomotive, are a popular paper collectible. Nearly all certificates have cancellation holes punched in them, indicating the stock has been redeemed. They are easy to find, the older ones being more valuable.

MUSEUMS

B & O Railroad Museum
Baltimore, Maryland 21223

Colorado Railroad Museum
Golden, Colorado 80401

Edaville Railroad Museum
South Carver, Massachusetts 02366

Illinois Railway Museum
Union, Illinois 60180

Lake Superior Transportation Museum
Duluth, Minnesota 55802

National Railroad Museum
Green Bay, Wisconsin 54304

Railroad Museum of Pennsylvania
Strasburg, Pennsylvania 17579

Smithsonian Institution
Washington, D.C. 20560

Valley Railroad Company
Essex, Connecticut 06426

COLLECTORS ORGANIZATIONS

National Association of Timetable Collectors
21 East Robin Road
Holland, Pennsylvania 18966

Railroadiana Collectors Association, Inc.
405 Byron Avenue
Mobile, Alabama 36609

BOOKS

Baker, Stanley L., *The Railroadiana Collector's Price Guide*. Hawthorn Books, Inc., 1977.

Baker, Stanley L., and Virginia Brainard Kunz, *The Collector's Book of Railroadiana*. Hawthorn Books, Inc., 1976.

Klamkin, Charles, *Railroadiana: The Collector's Guide to Railroad Memorabilia*. Funk & Wagnalls, 1976.

Redware
New Pottery for a New Country

The utilitarian pottery that is known as redware derives its name from the material it is made of: common clay with an iron content that causes it to turn red when fired. Because the clay is found almost everywhere and kitchen pottery is a necessity, this handmade, serviceable pottery was one of the first products to be manufactured in the New World and eventually it was produced almost everywhere in America.

Redware had a serious drawback: It was extremely porous; to be watertight it had to be glazed, generally with lead. As the *Pennsylvania Mercury* warned its readers in 1785, the lead "becomes a slow but sure poison" when the pottery is used for holding food or drink—particularly anything acidic.

Nevertheless, redware continued to be widely made for household use until more durable stoneware and imported whiteware replaced it around 1850. For larger

Wavy lines and a date were trailed onto the mug above with the liquid clay called slip. Slip decoration—especially if it includes names, dates or phrases—adds to value.

platters, storage jars, pitchers and mugs made as early as possible. Although a few pieces from before 1800 can be found and some relatively recent redware is very desirable *(page 47),* most collectors concentrate on items made during the first half of the 19th Century.

Much of this early-19th Century redware is plain and unglazed, as a flowerpot is. Such pieces are the easiest to find and the least valuable. Clear interior glazes, made of lead oxide, sand and water, add a bit to the value. Desirability of a piece depends also on the type and intricacy of the decoration—the more elaborate the better.

The simplest decoration in redware is an incised or impressed pattern. An awl or a comb was held alongside a piece while it turned on the potter's wheel, cutting into the damp clay to produce straight or wavy lines; for bands of stars or dots, a coggle wheel replaced the comb or awl.

The more skilled artisans experimented with color, using techniques common to potters the world over. In the easiest method, powdered oxides other than lead were mixed into the glaze. In the case of redware, oxides of manganese, iron or copper were used to obtain black, brown or green. But even this was time-consuming; also, the oxides were costly. For these reasons, colored glazes were used sparingly. Pieces with attractively colored exterior glazes are desirable, particularly if the decoration includes highlights such as smudges, splotches or daubs, which were applied by the potter before glazing.

A more effective, but also more difficult, decoration was applied by adding a white or colored liquid clay called slip directly to the piece, painting it on before glazing. This method called for considerable dexterity on the part of the potter. Slip had to be trickled, or trailed, onto unfired pottery from a small cup. The cup was pierced with one or more holes into which quills were inserted to serve as spouts and, as the cup was tilted, slip ran through the quills and onto the pottery. The

---

The collector, who wishes to remain anonymous, has been interested in redware for a number of years.

---

vessels, such as storage jars, the much harder stoneware was on hand. The inexpensive whiteware replaced redware on the table. Thus economic considerations, more than a concern for health, were responsible for the sharp decline in production. In a few places—particularly parts of Pennsylvania, North Carolina and the Shenandoah Valley of Virginia—the tradition of making redware persisted well into the 20th Century. In fact, redware is still being made, notably in North Carolina. In most areas, however, redware potters have been reduced to making tiles, bricks and flowerpots.

What redware collectors look for are jugs, pots, plates,

Although most redware containers were ordinary storage vessels, some were given unusual decoration such as the spider-like design on this rare 6 ½-inch jar of around 1850. The unglazed lid may not be the original.

Pots glazed only on the interior are fairly common. The yellow color on this 4 ½-inch example, probably made in Pennsylvania, is unusual.

Small, unadorned pieces such as this four-inch-tall pot are the easiest to find. Made around 1900, it is simply finished with a clear glaze.

mug pictured on page 35 was decorated in this manner with a single line of slip; the small plate with parallel wavy lines on page 41 was probably done with a two-quill cup. Potters seldom worked with more than three lines, but at least one plate still in existence was ornamented with 12 slip lines.

A third method of adding color, used on the redware now most eagerly sought, required the incising technique known as sgraffito, which seldom was applied to any other type of American pottery. For sgraffito decoration, a partially dry piece of redware was covered with slip, then the design was scratched through the slip to reveal the clay underneath. Pieces with sgraffito decoration were made mainly for show, sometimes to be displayed at home, sometimes to advertise a potter's work.

Either trailed slip or sgraffito adds greatly to the value of a piece, but the design that is created is also important. In general, representational forms are preferred to abstract patterns of lines and dots. Bird or flower motifs are popular with collectors, as are names, dates or phrases such as "hard times in Jersey." Potters in New England often marked the recipient's name in slip—"Sarahs dish" and "for Lucy" are typical—but many potters, especially in Pennsylvania, identified food instead, turning out plates labeled "mince pie" or "chicken potpie." A Pennsylvania potter named David Spinner once declared on a plate: "There is meat and sauerkraut. Our girl is a bride in the year 1810." Such lettered pieces of redware are among the most valued of all.

The intended use of the pottery also is important,

partly because some forms are rarer than others. Easiest to discover are jugs. Jars and pots come next in accessibility. Pitchers are hardest to find. In addition, the shape provides a clue to age. In jugs, pots, jars and similar containers, small bottoms and fat bodies are desirable because they usually indicate early manufacture.

Establishing a firm date for redware is more an art than a science, for the same materials have been used in much the same way for several centuries. One good clue is an obvious one. Old pieces of soft pottery should naturally show signs of wear and tear in the form of chips in the rim and perhaps even in the body; in addition, slip decoration should be clearly worn. A piece designed for kitchen work, such as a pie plate, will show its age.

Modern pieces imported from Latin America and elsewhere are marked with the place of manufacture, an identification that has been required by law since the turn of the century. Distinguishing the few late-19th Century examples and the rare 18th Century pieces from the bulk of redware of the early 1800s is difficult because the same styles and decorations remained in use. In addition to the telltale variations in shape, an evidence of age is the absence of glaze on the undersides of plates—underside glaze became common only toward the end of the 19th Century.

For related material, see the articles on Art Pottery, Belleek Porcelain, Bennington Pottery, Candleholders, Chinese Export Porcelain, Fiesta Ware, Majolica, Staffordshire, Stoneware and Wedgwood in separate volumes of this encyclopedia.

These two jars are similar in size—10 inches tall—and shape, but dissimilar in value. The jar on the left is worth four times as much as its companion because of the unusual flower decoration. The other jar, though older, is less valuable because its abstract design is more common.

Complex decoration makes this pitcher, 4 ½ inches tall, very desirable. The coating of white slip was probably put on for background, and was embellished with reddish lines and smudges before the pitcher was fired.

A Pennsylvania potter of the mid-19th Century splashed color onto this five-inch pitcher as exuberantly as abstract painter Jackson Pollock might have 100 years later. Splashed and sponged decoration is common; the use of two colors, however, is not.

Valuable for both its form and its design, this five-inch jug is one of the oldest pieces owned by the collector—it probably was made in the late 18th or early 19th Century. Its age is suggested by the egg shape, which is more common in early redware. Its white slip spots smudged with green make up a highly desirable color combination. The green is unusual because the coloring agent, copper oxide, was expensive.

Representational designs are sought after; the concentric suns make this notch-edged shallow plate more valuable than a similar plate with sim- *ple wavy lines or patterns. This plate, 13 inches in diameter, is believed to have been made in Huntington, New York.*

The unusual green streaks, as well as the wry inscription, make this 14-inch-wide platter extremely valuable. Copper oxide apparently ran down the slope of the dish during firing, creating an effect that may or may not have been intended.

Small plates like these, 4 ½ inches in diameter, are relatively difficult to find, and their value is much enhanced if they are decorated. The dish on the right is desirable for its two colors of slip in an unusual plaid design.

A water jar made at the Zuñi pueblo of New Mexico was acquired around 1880 by the first Indian agent assigned to that pueblo. The unusual arrangement of the Zuñi deer motif helps make this jar extremely valuable.

A desirable modern bowl with a carved water serpent was made at the Santa Clara pueblo by a technique that was perfected there during the 1930s.

Art of the Indian Potters

Three thousand years or so before the first European potter in America made the first turn of his wheel to shape a piece of redware, pottery was being made by many Indian tribes. After the advent of the white man, the Indians began to rely on bought or bartered utensils, and the potter's craft virtually died out everywhere except in the Southwest. Nevertheless, a tremendous variety of Indian pottery is available to the collector. Some, as it happens, is called redware, meaning only that it is red in color; it is not made of the same clay or in the same manner as the collectible discussed in the accompanying article. Redware, in contrast to Indian pottery, generally was made on a potter's wheel from a single lump of clay. Most Indian pottery was formed by building up coils of clay; the potter then thinned the walls and finally shaped and smoothed the object with a piece of gourd.

Collectors prize Indian pottery from all the thousands of years of its manufacture—Southwestern pottery from the early and middle years of the 20th Century as well as from the late 19th Century; earlier pottery from historic times; and a surprising number of well-preserved prehistoric pieces from various regions of the country. Buying or selling pottery made in prehistoric times, however, is now discouraged by professional archeologists and anthropologists who fear that trade in these artifacts will cause the loss of irreplaceable evidence of the past.

The Indians produced a variety of wares: vases, bowls, beakers, mugs, plates, pitchers, and single- and double-spouted jars. Regardless of form, the most desirable pottery—in many cases considered equal in value to prehistoric artifacts—is that produced in the Southwest since around 1900, when Indian crafts experienced a revival after many generations of decline.

The renaissance of Indian pottery owes much to the coming of the railroad in the 1880s. With the trains came tourists, some of whom began buying pots like the one pictured at left above. The pueblo women had maintained the tradition of making their own household wares, and many now became commercial potters.

At the turn of the century, pottery making was stimulated further by the archeological digs at Sikyatki in Arizona and the Pajarito Plateau excavations in New Mexico, which brought to light objects fashioned hundreds of years earlier by enormously talented and imaginative potters. These discoveries inspired a number of pueblo potters—notably Nampeyo of the Hano pueblo and Maria of San Ildefonso (who used various signatures)—to begin to create striking designs of their own in a number of forms. Nampeyo and Maria signed their later work, all of which is highly esteemed by collectors. Other valued pieces of pottery are those that bear the signature of Margaret Tafoya, Helen Cordero, Teresita Naranjo or Tony Da, Maria's grandson.

The large jar above, which displays the stylized bird found on much pottery from the Zia pueblo, is considered highly desirable and was probably made in the first decade of this century. The clay used by Zia potters is naturally brick-red in color.

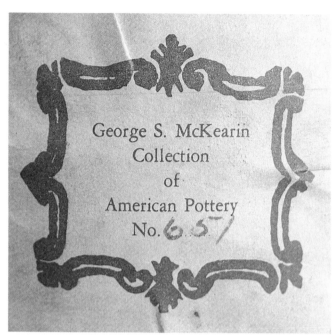

A label like the one above means that a piece to which it is affixed was once part of what was probably the most extensive collection of pottery, including redware, ever assembled in this country. The last of the George S. McKearin collection was sold after his death in 1958, and his label gives redware a cachet that collectors prize.

Three jugs made in New England share the plump egg shape characteristic of early pieces. The middle jug, 7 ½ inches tall, is the least valuable: Its shape is uneven and the color contrast is weak. The use of a rare color makes the jug on the left desirable. The equally desirable jug on the right is well made, with colors that indicate a New Hampshire origin. Contributing to the New Hampshire jug's value is its McKearin sticker (top), which indicates that it was once part of that famous collection.

A pot only 3 ½ inches tall (above) was made in the early 20th Century, possibly at the Honey Brook Pottery in Chester County, Pennsylvania. Similar pieces can be found easily.

Redware in animal or human shapes is generally desirable. However, this 3 ¾-inch-long salt shaker, made in North Carolina, dates only from the 1930s or '40s and is therefore less valuable than earlier examples.

This pitcher, six inches tall, has the colors of redware made in the Shenandoah Valley between 1860 and 1900. Many Shenandoah pitchers of that period are more elongated than pieces made elsewhere.

This 7 ½-inch pitcher is attributed to Jacob Medinger, a Pennsylvania potter who died in 1932. Because they are recent, Medinger's pieces are not hard to find, but his fine craftsmanship makes them desirable.

This slip-decorated plate from the Moravian community in Salem, North Carolina, is one of the rarest pieces the collector owns. Probably made by master potter Rudolph Christ, it is 11 inches in diameter and has a lively design in three colors skillfully executed in trailed slip. Although many redware plates were molded, Moravian plates like this one were thrown on a potter's wheel.

This 9 ½-inch Pennsylvania plate is an example of sgraffito—the technique of scratching a slip-covered piece to expose the clay underneath. Sgraffito is extremely valuable. Many of the surviving pieces were made by German settlers and bear inscriptions in their native language.

Coin banks in the shape of fruits and vegetables are a popular form of redware, but not many survive, since they were likely to be broken for withdrawals. These six banks from the late 19th Century rest in a red-ware milk pan made some 50 years earlier. In increasing order of rarity and collectible value they are an orange, an apple, a pear, a peach, a tomato and a squash. The squash is glazed, all the others painted.

MUSEUMS

The Brooklyn Museum
Brooklyn, New York 11238

Litchfield Historical Society and Museum
Litchfield, Connecticut 06759

Mercer Museum of the Bucks County
Historical Society
Doylestown, Pennsylvania 18901

The New-York Historical Society
New York, New York 10024

Old Salem, Inc.
Winston-Salem, North Carolina 27108

Old Sturbridge Village
Sturbridge, Massachusetts 01566

Pennsylvania Farm Museum
Lancaster, Pennsylvania 17601

Philadelphia Museum of Art
Philadelphia, Pennsylvania 19101

Smithsonian Institution
Washington, D.C. 20560

BOOKS

Barber, Edwin Atlee, *Tulip Ware of the Pennsylvania-German Potters.* Dover Publications, Inc., 1970.

Bivins, John, Jr., *The Moravian Potters in North Carolina.* University of North Carolina Press, 1972.

James, Arthur E., *The Potters and Potteries of Chester County, Pennsylvania.* Schiffer Publishing Ltd., 1978.

Lasansky, Jeannette, *Central Pennsylvania Redware Pottery.* Union County Oral Traditions Projects, Court House, Lewisburg, Pennsylvania, 1979.

Powell, Elizabeth A., *Pennsylvania Pottery, Tools and Processes.* The Bucks County Historical Society, 1972.

Stradling, Diana and J. Garrison, eds., *The Art of the Potter.* Main Street/Universe Books, 1977.

Watkins, Lura Woodside:
Early New England Potters and Their Wares. Archon Books, 1968.
Early New England Pottery. Old Sturbridge Village, 1966.

Rock and Roll Memorabilia
From Rhythm and Blues to Woodstock

As a 13-year-old rock and roll expert in 1957, I considered recordings such as "Rock around the Clock" by Bill Haley and the Comets or Little Richard's "Tutti Frutti" as nothing more than relics of ancient history, even then of interest only to collectors of rock and roll memorabilia. After all, those tunes were already two years old. Dating from the early 1950s, rock and roll music may have created the youngest of all collectibles. It also may well be the subject that has generated the greatest number of collectible categories for each of its years of existence.

The rapid development of rock and roll makes the music impossible to define succinctly. Although most rock and roll music can be identified by an insistent beat, its evolution is marked by a bewildering kaleidoscope of styles performed by fancifully named vocal and instrumental groups.

After World War II, urban black music called rhythm and blues was adopted by white youths. In 1951 Alan

---

Ralph M. Newman has been editor of The Time Barrier Express, a collectors' magazine, and produced a rock and roll radio show.

Freed, a Cleveland disc jockey, popularized the name "rock and roll" by combining two bits of slang that were prominent in rhythm and blues lyrics. In 1954 Elvis Presley began to remake this sound by combining it with country music.

By the early 1960s Motown Records, a black company in Detroit, was teaching America a new meaning for the word "soul." In 1963 the Beatles arrived on the scene with a style that swept all before them. A short six years later some half a million fans were swaying to the so-called acid rock at the three-day concert at Woodstock, New York, that is generally accepted as a cultural turning point. Woodstock serves many collectors as a cutoff point for early rock and roll memorabilia. Collectibles come from all of these periods and per-

A button from the 1950s (above) proclaiming allegiance to the teen-age world's new sound is typical of collectibles fairly easy to find.

formers, and they include a great variety of recordings, artifacts, magazines and posters, especially those that are associated with Elvis Presley and the Beatles.

Because rock and roll is mainly recorded music, recordings are the chief type of collectible—especially 45 rpm singles, the seven-inch discs with a silver-dollar-sized hole in the middle, which were introduced in 1949. They are singles because they have one tune on each side and 45s because they play at 45 revolutions per minute. Some songs from the rhythm and blues period were issued only on the 10-inch, 78 rpm records that preceded the 45s, but most rhythm and blues recordings exist in both types.

By the early 1960s the 78 rpm discs had disappeared from the market, and the rock and roll music of subsequent periods was issued on 45s and 33⅓s. When a collectible rhythm and blues song is available in both 45 and 78 rpm versions, the former commands about twice the price of the 78.

The rarer the record and the better its condition, the higher its value as a collectible. Rarity is based on the particular record itself, not on the tune it carries. For example, the 1958 song "Book of Love," recorded by a group inaccurately called the Monotones, sold relatively few copies on its original Mascot label release (No. 124), but it became a smash hit when the same recording was reissued by Argo (No. 5290). The Mascot disc is worth five times as much as the Argo.

A difference in collectible value can be created by small variations in the labels. When Dootone originally released the Penguins' "Earth Angel" in 1955, it was such a huge hit that pressing plants exhausted their supply of the original red labels and had to use black, ma-

Featured on a 1956 poster announcing one of Hollywood's early low-budget rock and roll movies is Alan Freed, the self-proclaimed inventor of rock and roll. In 1951, as a Cleveland disc jockey, he first brought the name for the music to public attention.

Rhythm and blues discs from the early and mid-1950s are the quarry of many collectors. The 45 rpm discs pictured above, by the Moonglows, Duces of Rhythm & Tempo Toppers, and the Flamingos, all black groups, are rare; the Platters' "Only You" is rare on the Federal label, but it was a smash hit as a Mercury re-recording. The records by the "5" Royales and the Cadillacs were hits and so are not rare.

Early rock and roll by white musicians is represented by the three 45s shown above. The Bill Haley disc from 1953 is considered by many the first true rock and roll record. Carl Perkins' first disc, "Movie Magg" is a great rarity. One of Buddy Holly's first discs, "Love Me" is fairly rare as a sample given to disc jockeys. Haley had a string of hits, including "Rock around the Clock"; Perkins had only one — "Blue Suede Shoes."

roon and blue as well. A collector who wants to acquire the most valuable one will have to find the red label; the collector who is interested in having everything can look for all four of them.

The greatest number of rock and roll rarities come from the rhythm and blues era because the 45 rpm records were issued in small quantities. Names of groups from this period make up special categories. Among those whose records are sought are a number of groups with bird names—in addition to the Penguins there were the Flamingos, the Orioles, the Robins, the Swallows, the Crows, the Cardinals, the Ravens and the Meadowlarks. Desirable also are fives—the Five Keys, the "5" Royales, the Five Satins—as well as at least one four, the Four Tunes, and automotive names, such as the El Dorados and the Cadillacs.

Very rare are the Flamingos' "I Really Don't Want to Know" on Parrot (No. 811) and the Five Keys' "Red Sails in the Sunset" on Aladdin (No. 3127). The rarest is a record in rhythm and blues style of "Stormy Weather," by the Five Sharps on the Jubilee label (No. 5104). Only two copies are known; one that turned up in California in a box of old 78s—the whole box was bought for about two dollars—was sold in 1977 for $3,866.

The rarities of the period following rhythm and blues are records that were cut by famous artists at the beginning of their careers. Five of the best-known rock and roll collectibles are the discs Elvis Presley cut for Sun Records in Memphis during 1954 and 1955. These recordings are worth 10 to 15 times as much as the same recordings reissued under the RCA label. The Beatles' earliest recording, even rarer, is Decca No. 31382, "My Bonnie," a flop when it was originally issued in 1962. Curiously, the pink-label version made for disc jockeys is worth only about a third as much as the regular issue bearing a black label, although disc-jockey records are ordinarily the more valuable.

Old records and a variety of related artifacts are the stock in trade of thrift shops, secondhand stores, yard sales and even some record stores. The most comprehensive sources, however, are specialized dealers and the collectors' periodicals (page 63) that provide listings of mail auctions.

Among the things that collectors are likely to find fairly easily are Elvis Presley purses, shoes, skirts, scarves, T-shirts, wallets and hats (page 55), as well as costume jewelry. An autograph of Presley's is also easy to find—and inexpensive to buy—because he gave so many. Fans of the Beatles have a similar range of goods to collect, at similar prices. Unique Beatles collectibles are the original drawings, called cels, from their animated movie, Yellow Submarine.

Two popular kinds of rock and roll memorabilia have broader appeal. These are fan magazines from the

CHUCK BERRY   CHUCK BERRY MUSIC, Inc.
Berry Park
Wentzville, Missouri

Publicity pictures, such as this one of the great writer-performer Chuck Berry, are desirable. Berry composed and recorded many hits, including "Maybellene," "Sweet Little Sixteen" and "Johnny B. Goode."

1950s and '60s—*Teen Talk, Cheetah, 16* and *Teen Pin-Ups,* to name a few—and posters advertising rock and roll concerts and movies.

Posters for rock and roll movies—a cinematic genre that started in 1956 with *Rock, Rock, Rock (page 51)* and *Rock around the Clock*—have come to be regarded by knowledgeable collectors as underpriced bargains. Rock and roll concert posters, which originated during the '50s and were produced all through the 1960s in large quantity, are considered particularly desirable for their art work. They were zealously collected at the time, and many of them still survive.

Rock and roll posters of the late '60s, with their dazzlingly colored drug-oriented abstractions, are a far cry from the 1950s advertisements that showed rock and roll stars dressed in coats and ties. The gap between them is little more than a handful of years—but for a collector of rock and roll they are years of excitement and innovation.

For related material, see the articles on Country Music, Jazz Memorabilia, Jukeboxes, Movie Memorabilia and Posters in separate volumes of The Encyclopedia of Collectibles.

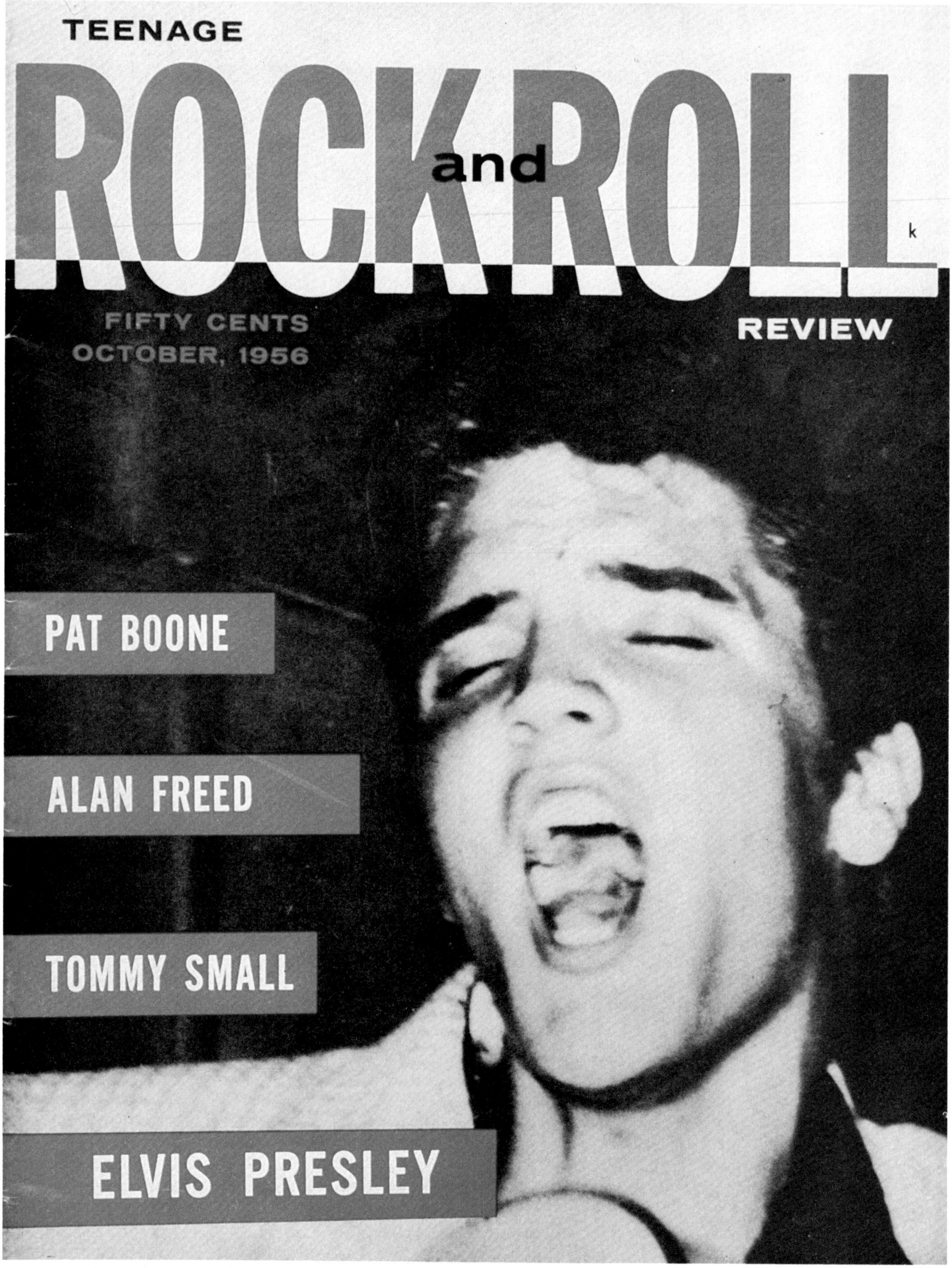

TEENAGE
ROCK and ROLL
REVIEW

FIFTY CENTS
OCTOBER, 1956

k

PAT BOONE

ALAN FREED

TOMMY SMALL

ELVIS PRESLEY

The cover of the magazine shown above displays Elvis Presley in 1956, the year he achieved world-wide fame. He shares the inside pages with other rock and roll stars, which makes this issue less desirable than those that were devoted exclusively to him.

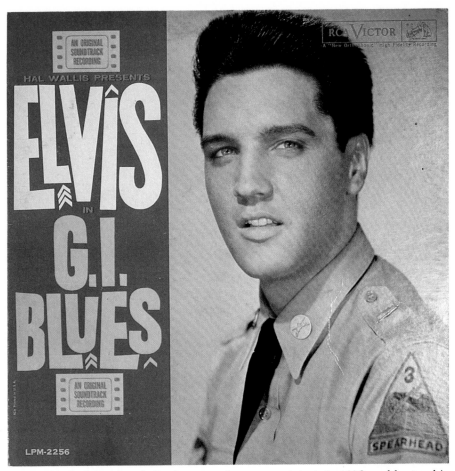

A Memphis draft board made Presley a very famous army private in 1958, and he stayed in uniform for the 1960 movie G.I. Blues. This sound-track album is collectible but not hard to find.

The first commercial record made by Presley attracted no national attention when it was released in 1954. Now it is one of rock and roll's most prized collectibles.

A fan-club membership card—the one shown is the collector's—and an advertisement for lipstick are among the paper ephemera that came out of Presley's career.

This example of a porkpie hat with an extra-wide hatband celebrating Presley's early hits has particular value because the manufacturer's tag is still attached.

Easiest to find of the rock and roll recordings of the 1950s are those, like the three above and at left, made to play at 45 rpm's. The examples pictured are notable partly for their stars —Fats Domino, who brought a Louisiana Cajun accent to his songs; the Everly Brothers, an immensely successful duo who performed in a style known as country rock; and Chubby Checker, the Twist King. The records by Domino and by the Everly Brothers are EPs, or extended-play 45s —meaning that they had two songs to a side, instead of the usual one.

Rock and roll LP records from the 1950s are fairly rare. The five at right and opposite offer a cross section of the music as it sounded at the end of the decade. Gene Vincent was Capitol Records' moderately successful answer to Elvis Presley's popularity; Little Richard was a rock and roll pioneer; the Cadets were a rhythm and blues group; and the Impalas and the Champs were among the first groups to associate the music with automobile and motorcycle speed.

Beatles buttons bloomed on blouses and coat lapels when the quartet first appeared in America in 1964. Collectors can assemble a variety of tin memorabilia like this at little cost.

A collector who finds a worn pair of Beatles sneakers owns nothing more than some old shoes. However, a pair like these in unworn condition could bring as much as $25.

A four-inch-tall set of the Beatles —George, John, Ringo and Paul —in painted plaster, with their oversized heads on springs, originally sold for five dollars in 1966 and brought three times that amount a decade later.

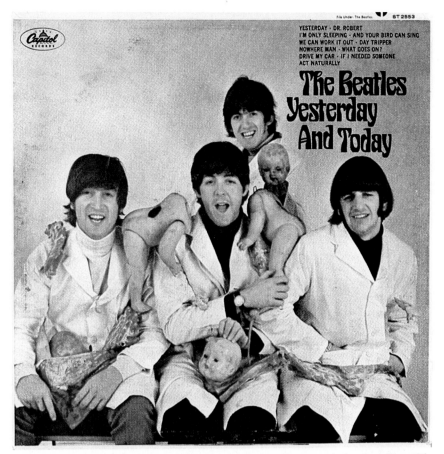

The Beatles record in this cover, the original, is known to collectors as the butcher album. The cover was quickly withdrawn when retailers objected that it was in bad taste, and few survive.

This early Beatles hit appeared first with a white label (top) and then, when sales acceler-ated, with a black label, on which the slogan Don't drop out was added to urge young peo-ple to stay in school. The white-label disc is 10 times as valuable as the black.

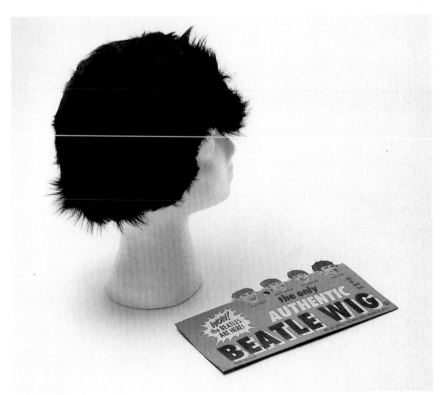

The Beatles' hair style—widely known as the mop top—was a trademark. To achieve instant shagginess, many fans bought Beatle wigs like the one above, now rare collectibles.

A psychedelic portrayal of Bob Dylan on the cover gives extra value to a 1966 issue of Crawdaddy, a magazine of rock and roll news and commentary. Crawdaddy is collected both for the value of its criticism and for the quality of its cover art.

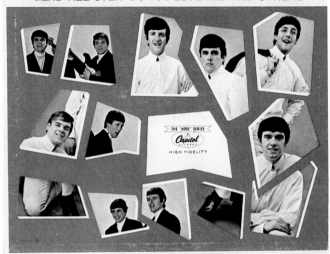

These albums are reminders of directions taken by rock and roll in the 1960s: the Dave Clark Five was in the vanguard of the English invasion; Diana Ross and the Supremes, and the Temptations were stars of the Detroit sound; the Beach Boys were noted for surfing songs.

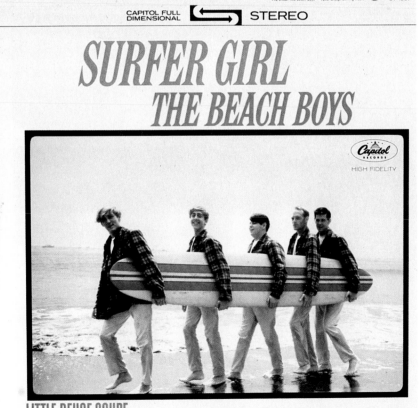

This 1968 poster for a Jimi Hendrix acid-rock concert in San Francisco used designs meant to suggest drug-induced hallucinations.

The paper sleeve of this Rolling Stones hit single, showing the group dressed in an odd assortment of women's clothes, is much more valuable than the record inside.

A Rolling Stones tour book—an illustrated chronicle of one of the group's earliest nationwide appearances in concert—is a memento that is fairly easy to find.

Tickets and a button from the Woodstock festival have little intrinsic value, but great personal meaning for the 500,000 people who for three days turned the small town into the world capital of rock and roll.

PERIODICALS
Goldmine, Arena Magazine Company, Fraser, Michigan 48026

Record Exchanger, Vintage Records, Box 6144, Orange, California 92667

The Time Barrier Express, Time Barrier Express Enterprises, Inc., Box 206, Yonkers, New York 10710

BOOKS
Hill, Randal C., *The Official Price Guide to Collectible Rock Records.* House of Collectibles, 1979.

Nite, Norm N.:
Rock On: The Illustrated Encyclopedia of Rock n' Roll. The Solid Gold Years. Thomas Y. Crowell Co., Inc., 1974.
Rock On: The Illustrated Encyclopedia of Rock n' Roll. The Modern Years: 1964-Present, Thomas Y. Crowell Co., Inc., 1978.

COMING TO THE PARSON

Rogers Groups
Little Stories in Plaster

Hoping to find a set of matched lamps, my family and I walked into an antique store one day and came away with our first Rogers group, one of the plaster sculptures of 19th Century scenes now so popular with collectors. Later we were driving past a furniture store in suburban Long Island when our son yelled, "Hey, there's a Rogers group!" We stopped and went in to look. We found not one but several groups offered for sale—as makeshift lamps. They were badly chipped, but we bought them for a fraction

Herman Deutsch, a Long Island accountant, began collecting Rogers groups with his wife, Eleanor, and son, Sam, in 1961.

of what they have been worth since we restored them—a process that these collectibles lend themselves to.

Other collectors report similar experiences. One couple stopped at a farmhouse to ask if there were any antiques for sale. The farmer led them to a chicken coop. Inside the couple discovered 12 Rogers groups serving as perches for hens. This couple also found several groups in a neglected corner of a warehouse; they were told they could have them for 50 cents a pound.

Although the 80 or so different scenes reproduced by John Rogers and his employees weigh an average of about 50 pounds each, any one is worth considerably more than the per-pound rate. Known as Rogers groups almost from the beginning, these sculptures captured scenes from everyday life, more than somewhat idealized and often lightly made fun of. They were immensely popular in Victorian times, then went out of fashion until lovers of Americana rediscovered them in the 1960s. Because they can be mended if damaged, condition counts for less than rarity in determining value.

One of the rarest, and therefore among the most valuable, is a group with two men on horses entitled *Polo*. Only five copies are known to exist. In 1975 one sold for $10,000, a good deal more than is commanded by other rare groups such as *The Slave Auction* and *The Bushwhacker*, each of which exists in fewer than 15 copies. On the

John Rogers' depiction of a young couple and a minister discussing wedding plans, which sold 8,000 copies, includes a typically wry note: a hostile dog and cat to express a skeptical view of married life.

other hand, the group pictured opposite, *Coming to the Parson*, was enormously popular, so many were made and sold; in the late 1970s examples went for less than $400. Most Rogers groups are worth a little more than that but a lot less than *Polo*.

The Slave Auction was the sculpture that established John Rogers as a sculptor-businessman. Born in Massachusetts in 1829, he was plagued by eyesight too poor to let him pursue his chosen career as an engineer. By accident he discovered that he had a knack for constructing figures out of clay and bits of wood, and that his limited vision did not affect his modeling. Working at various jobs, he moved from city to city, in his spare time sculpting in clay 50 or so forerunners of his groups. Although he went to Paris and Rome for a year to study academic sculpture, when he returned to the United States sculpture was still just a hobby.

In Chicago, where he was working as a draftsman, he was asked by some friends to make something for a church bazaar. He produced a scene of two men playing checkers—a favorite subject. (One version can be seen on page 67.) As a raffle prize, the piece was a success—300 tickets sold at a quarter each—convincing Rogers that he could make a living as a designer and merchandiser of mass-produced sculptures.

He moved to New York and produced *The Slave Auction*. It was 1859, a year before the Civil War started, and the timing no less than the effectiveness of the portrayal drew attention. At first stores refused to display so forthright a condemnation of slavery. (The auctioneer's hair simulated the devil's horns.) Even after Rogers hired a black salesman to sell the piece on the streets of New York and abolitionists took it up, it did not sell well.

Rogers' next efforts were more successful. From the outset he was sales-minded. Whenever he could, he arranged for stores to display groups in their most prominent windows. He gave pieces to newspaper editors in exchange for a feature story or a free advertisement. Later he bought advertisements in magazines and newspapers and regularly published a catalogue for mail orders. Rogers groups were photographed for stereopticon cards, which gave a three-dimensional view, for the *carte de visite* pictures that Victorians collected, and for slides for magic-lantern shows.

Traveling Magician, a sculpture that is relatively rare, could be viewed from the front (right) or back (above) to get a behind-the-scenes demonstration of how a dove was being readied to follow the rabbit out of the hat. The models for the children in this sculpture were Rogers' own son and daughter.

Favorable publicity apparently came easily. Of one of Rogers' War subjects Union General Joseph Hawley was quoted as saying, "Nothing relating to the war in painting or sculpture surpasses" it. And that famous Indian fighter George Armstrong Custer was photographed in his living quarters in Dakota Territory with two Rogers groups on his desk: *Wounded to the Rear/One More Shot* and *Mail Day*. (The general's widow, in her memoir, *Boots and Saddles*, complained about the chore of lugging the plaster sculptures from post to post.)

The publicity and the sales promotion paid off. Over a period of 33 years Rogers produced somewhere between 70,000 and 80,000 copies of his sculptures. Prices ranged from five dollars to $50, averaging $14. Most sculptures are about two feet high.

Rogers began each group with a rough sketch. Then he produced a model in clay. The model usually was cast in bronze and hand-finished to serve as a pattern. These patterns are also very valuable. To make a mold for the figures, Rogers' workmen poured glue over the bronze pattern in sections and allowed the glue to dry. Each section of dried glue, after being pulled off the pattern, served as a mold into which plaster was poured. The separate plaster castings were joined with wires, then the joints were smoothed over with paste. After the castings had dried for a week, coats of zinc white and burnt umber mixed with linseed oil and turpentine were applied.

Despite efforts to make the plaster sculptures sturdy, chipping and breakage were common. Rogers foresaw this problem; he offered repair instructions and sold kits for touch-up coloring. Many modern collectors follow Rogers' advice, restoring chipped or broken groups, which sell for less than half the value they would have if whole. Our son, Sam, started his collection this way, buying broken groups disdained by others. Today his restored pieces make up a valuable collection.

Restoration is relatively easy but time-consuming. If pieces are missing, a mold must be made of the missing part, using a complete group. Collectors are usually glad to help one another by allowing a mold to be taken. Dental impression material is best to use because it sets quickly and can be peeled off after the plaster hardens.

If condition is not the crucial consideration in collecting Rogers groups, authenticity is. Some duplicates are very valuable. Copies were made during Rogers' lifetime, probably in England or France. These were cast not in plaster but in parian, a marbled white porcelain that shrinks slightly as it cools, making the copies smaller than the originals. Collectors prize the copies because parian is more durable than plaster; parian castings are rare and are valued accordingly.

Imitations—groups made by such Rogers competitors as Caspar Hennecke Co. of Milwaukee, J. J. West of Chicago, and Jonathan Hartley and Samuel Conkey of New York—also are valued by some collectors. There are at least two ways to distinguish these Rogers-like groups from authentic Rogers sculptures. With one exception, Rogers' own works are marked on the base, in capital letters, with the title and "John Rogers, New York." The exception is an early work, *The Bath*, which bears the title but not the signature. A second clue to authenticity is the iris of the eye; in a Rogers group it is recessed, not in relief as is usual in imitations.

Rogers had his greatest popularity from the start of the Civil War through the 1880s. At affairs called Rogers parties people put white powder on their hands and faces and posed in attitudes of different Rogers groups. People who could not afford to buy a group bought a picture of one. *Coming to the Parson* became *the* wedding present. Fashionable physicians deemed a Rogers group on a medical theme essential for their reception rooms.

Suddenly, toward the end of the 19th Century, the groups came to seem naïve, sentimental and simpleminded. Rogers made little effort to reverse the trend. When he retired in 1893 he was content that his groups had remained popular for more than 30 years.

Rogers' second-best seller, after Coming to the Parson, was this version of a checkers game, for which his wife modeled the onlooker. One of four depictions of the pastime, it is entitled Checkers Up at the Farm.

In Neighboring Pews, according to an exegesis by Rogers, the younger of two late-arriving ladies is shown the place in the hymnbook while her companion betrays indignation over the gentleman's preference.

Auf Wiedersehen is found in several variations. This one, distinguished by the fact that the boy wears a hat and is not waving a handkerchief, was made between 1950 and 1955 and is very desirable.

Best known of all Hummels is the Merry Wanderer, which has also been issued in more sizes than any other. This is the common 1972 version, 9½ inches high. The 29-inch version, which was issued in 1969, is particularly valuable.

HUMMEL TRADEMARKS

Below are some Hummel trademarks and the periods in which they were most often used. Until 1950 a crown symbol accompanied the "WG" of the manufacturer, W. Goebel Porzellanfabrik. The bee (Hummel means "bumblebee") in a V (for Verkaufsgesellschaft, "distribution company") appeared in 1950 and became smaller and more stylized in the 1950s and 1960s. Beginning in 1972 it was set over the name. The facsimile signature of Sister Maria Innocentia Hummel appears on all figurines.

1935-1949	1950-1955
1956-1959	W. Germany 1960-1963
© by W. Goebel W. Germany 1964-1972	Goebel W. Germany 1972

Schoolgirls was made only in this 9 ½-inch size until the mid-1960s, when a 7 ½-inch version was added. The larger is the more valuable.

A Nun's Porcelain Children

When American soldiers stationed in Germany after World War II began looking for gifts to send the folks back home, they found on post-exchange shelves charmingly winsome figurines, called Hummels, like the ones pictured here. The folks back home loved them—so much that they set off a collecting craze of remarkable intensity. Examples similar to *Schoolgirls (above, right)*, which the PX sold for about $10 in the early 1960s, soon multiplied in value 100 times or more.

The porcelain children that inspired this rage have an unlikely origin. They are made by a well-known pottery firm, W. Goebel Porzellanfabrik of Rodental, Bavaria. But the designs are based on drawings by Sister Maria Innocentia Hummel, a German nun who died at the age of 37 in 1946. She had studied art in Munich before she entered the Franciscan convent at Siessen in southern Germany, and her superiors encouraged her to continue drawing and painting.

Convent-issued postcards showing the child subjects she made her specialty came to the attention of the Goebel company, which won permission to create figurines based on her drawings. The convent receives royalties from the sales and must approve the designs. Hundreds of Hummel wares have been made since the first was sold in 1935; besides figurines there are plates, candleholders, ashtrays, holy-water fonts, plaques, dinner bells, music boxes, lamp bases and dolls.

The value of a Hummel depends partly on its subject but more on its age and rarity. However, few figurines are dated, and many of the designs have remained in production over long periods—some of the most popular, such as the *Merry Wanderer (opposite, bottom)*, were reissued at intervals. Others have been reissued with slight modifications—colors altered, flowers added, socks changed. Knowledge of variations helps identification, and date of manufacture can be established roughly from the style of trademark *(above, left)*.

Rogers used three of his children—Johnny, Katie and Charlie—as models for the group at left. It is a moderately expensive item.

A rare unsigned group, The Bath (above) was probably sculpted in 1870 but not issued until 1894, after Rogers' retirement, perhaps because the near-nudity of the little boy seemed improper at the time.

A depiction of a teacher enraptured with one of the older pupils in his one-room school was a popular sculpture and is easy to find.

FETCHING THE DOCTOR

*For his equestrian groups Rogers brought horses into the studio to draw from. This one shows a
doctor making a hurried house call after being summoned by a little boy.*

The sculpture above, depicting an escaped black slave helping a wounded white scout back to safety, is not the mass-produced plaster casting widely sold but a bronze that was specially made. It is accordingly valuable.

One of Rogers' most admired sculptures portrays a Southern woman drawing rations for her family after taking a Union loyalty oath. This design is fairly easy to find.

This is one of three variations, all sought after, of President Abraham Lincoln conferring with General U. S. Grant (left) and Secretary of War Edwin Stanton. Lincoln's son Robert regarded it, a biographer wrote, "as the most lifelike portrait of his father in sculpture."

The legend of John Alden and Priscilla was recorded (above) with a literalism that extended to using the characters' names on the base. Extra detail was captured by casting the spinning wheel of pewter, not plaster.

Actor Joseph Jefferson posed for this sculpture in one of his most famous roles—as Bob Acres in Richard Brinsley Sheridan's comedy The Rivals. One of the last statues that Rogers made, it is rare.

Rogers' first attempts at portraying Shakespearean scenes did not sell well, but this scene from The Merchant of Venice, made midway in his career, was commercially as well as artistically successful.

The three sons Rogers used as models for this statue all failed to make the Yale football team. The fourth model, William Corbin, became captain of that team. The group is exceedingly rare.

MUSEUMS
John Rogers Studio and Museum
New Canaan, Connecticut 06840

Lightner Museum
City Hall Museum Complex, King Street
St. Augustine, Florida 32084

The New-York Historical Society
New York, New York 10024

Pioneer Village
Minden, Nebraska 68959

The Vermont Country Store
Rockingham, Vermont 05101

COLLECTORS ORGANIZATIONS
The Rogers Group
13 Oenoke Ridge
New Canaan, Connecticut 06840

BOOKS
Bleier, Paul and Meta, *John Rogers' Groups of Statuary*. Published by the authors, North Woodmere, New York, 1976.

Smith, Mr. and Mrs. Chetwood, *Rogers Groups: Thought and Wrought by John Rogers*. Charles Goodspeed, 1934.

Wallace, David H., *John Rogers, the People's Sculptor*. Wesleyan University Press, 1967.

THE FOUR GENERATIONS OF OUR ROYAL FAMILY

COPYRIGHT DESIGN, ENT. STA. HALL

Royal Souvenirs
Mementos of the Ruling Family

The last ruling monarch of Egypt, King Farouk, is reported to have forecast that only five royal families would eventually survive in the modern world: diamonds, spades, hearts, clubs—and the House of Windsor. His prophecy has yet to come to pass—there are still many crowned heads around the world—but, insofar as collectors of royal souvenirs are concerned, Farouk was right. Even though commemoratives of other royal families are sought, most American collectors concentrate on those of Britain's monarchy. The births, marriages, investitures, coronations, tours and jubilees of the House of Windsor have been

---

Larry Calvert, wardrobe supervisor of a theatrical company, began collecting as a child by saving clippings about King George VI.

---

marked by the production of decorated tinware and chinaware, toys, flags, dolls, neckties, socks, statuettes, soap, buttons and, most widely collected, ceramic mugs.

Examples of almost all royal souvenirs can be found for just a few dollars. The best bargains are in flea markets. While visiting one near my home, I found a pair of three-inch-tall plaster figures of Queen Elizabeth II and Prince Philip dated 1947, the year of their marriage. I paid about 1/10 the price a dealer would have charged.

My find was valuable because it was a pair and because it was made right after World War II, when few souvenirs were manufactured. Such considerations aside, the value of a royal souvenir is determined by age. A mug honoring Queen Victoria, for example, will bring half as much again as one for her grandson George V.

Pre-Victorian commemoratives—the first apparently is a medal celebrating Edward VI's coronation in 1547 —are exceedingly rare. Even the earliest souvenirs of Queen Victoria, whose 64-year reign marks the starting point for most collections, are hard to find because few were made. Some of the most sought after bear her full name—Alexandrina Victoria. It was assumed that when she took the throne she would use the first name. When

she came to sign her first official paper, however, the 18-year-old monarch wrote "Victoria" in a firm hand.

Equally rare are the first commemoratives of her 1840 marriage to Prince Albert. But by late 1841 individual portraits of the pair and their children or of the family group were being put on china. There are no souvenirs of Victoria's Silver Jubilee—she was in seclusion after Albert's death in 1861 and no celebration was held. But souvenirs of her 1887 Golden Jubilee are relatively easy to find, and those of the 1897 Diamond Jubilee, the 60th anniversary of her accession, are even more common.

Victoria's successor, Edward VII, spent most of his long life as the Prince of Wales. His reign lasted only nine years, and as a result souvenirs of him as King are generally scarcer than those of his years as a prince.

The opposite is true of the two Georges who followed Edward VII; both were second sons, and their early years were largely ignored by makers of souvenirs. George VI's daughter Elizabeth II was an infrequent subject of commemoratives until her father became King. However, her heir, Prince Charles, was a common subject in his youth, and souvenirs of him, like those of Elizabeth II's 1977 Silver Jubilee, are easily found.

Of all 20th Century royalty, it is Edward VIII whose commemoratives are most sought. When he abdicated to marry Mrs. Wallis Simpson just before his planned coronation, huge quantities of souvenirs were already in production. Their makers feared a disastrous trade loss. Instead, the public avidly bought premature commemoratives of the canceled coronation, and they remain popular today. The same applies to abdication souvenirs— and to the commemoratives of the coronation of his successor, George VI. Many of them were simply adapted from designs originally planned for Edward VIII.

Manufacturers were not the only ones thrown into confusion by the abdication. The day had already been picked for the coronation; the crowned heads of Europe, leaders of the Commonwealth countries and foreign heads of state had arranged to attend. It was too late to change. So on May 12, 1937, the coronation took place with the same guests and the same pageantry. Only the monarch was different and only the Archbishop of Canterbury, who placed the crown on George VI's head and declared him King, had to learn new lines.

Valued for its good condition, a tin plate portrays four royal generations: Queen Victoria, son Edward VII (top left), grandson George V (top right) and great-grandson Edward VIII. The plate commemorates Victoria's 60th year on the throne.

This china perfume bottle, from Victoria's Golden Jubilee, is desirable for the mark of the Royal Worcester Porcelain Company.

A stoneware gin flask is a rare souvenir. In a style resembling a medieval stone carving, it depicts Victoria in coronation regalia at the time of her 1837 accession to the throne.

A Diamond Jubilee medal of Celluloid is unusual because it was made in America. It bears the names of its once-thriving Anglophile sponsors, the British Societies of Philadelphia and neighboring Camden, New Jersey.

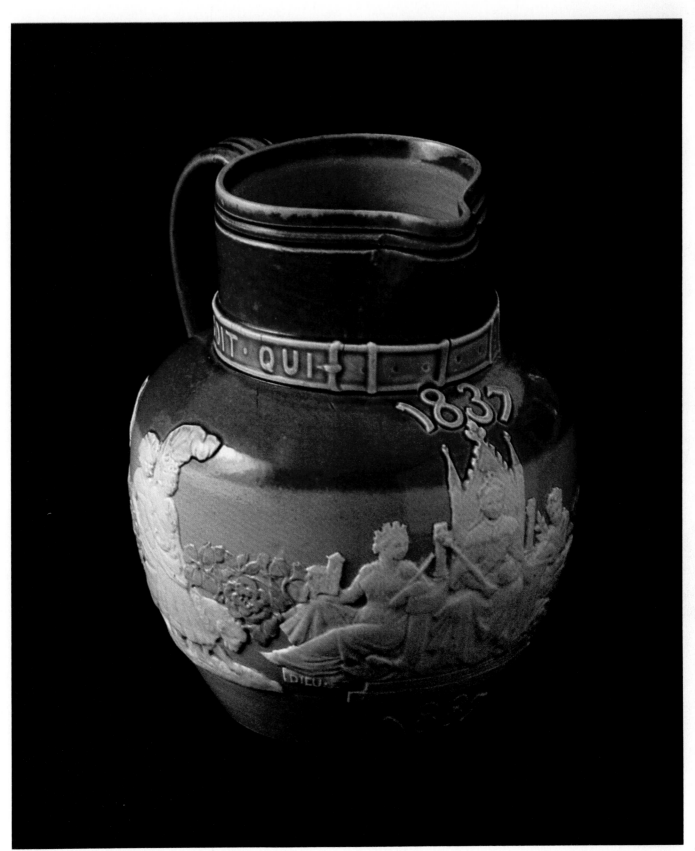

Commemorating Victoria's Golden Jubilee in 1887, a rare stoneware jug has a royal motto on a band around the neck, her accession date be- *low the spout. The design—figures celebrating the arts, industry, peace and empire—appears also on vases and beakers, which are equally rare.*

A pin tray commemorating Edward VII's 1902 coronation is easy to find. The picture depicting him and his queen, Alexandra, was also used on other items.

This pressed-glass creamer is a common souvenir of Edward's 1888 silver wedding anniversary. By then he was 46 years old, but still Prince of Wales.

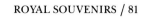

The china plate at left depicting George V and Queen Mary, from his coronation in 1911, is sought after both as a coronation souvenir and as a marked piece of Royal Doulton porcelain.

An eggcup is a desirable souvenir of the Silver Jubilee of George V in 1935. Most of the chinaware made to mark such occasions was in the form of regular cups and plates.

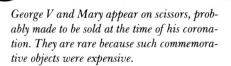

George V and Mary appear on scissors, probably made to be sold at the time of his coronation. They are rare because such commemorative objects were expensive.

A well-preserved 1929 calendar shows a debonair Prince of Wales in the period when he was familiar worldwide as the handsome epitome of youthful royalty. The future Edward VIII also appeared, in Army uniform, on a similar 1928 calendar and it, too, is prized.

A brass ornament for a horse's harness marks Edward VIII's 1911 investiture as Prince of Wales. The ostrich feathers are part of the crest for that title, and they appear on souvenirs of other Princes of Wales.

The tin button above at left prematurely celebrates Edward's aborted coronation. The other button notes—appropriately in Welsh—his investiture as Prince of Wales at Caernarvon Castle.

The lion handles and the elephants in the design of the mugs above identify both as the work of British artist Laura Knight, famed for circus

paintings. The one on the left was done for Edward VIII's coronation, then modified (right) for the abdication. The latter is more valuable.

A nine-inch-long coronation coach —a cookie tin meant to be used as a toy after the cookies were eaten —is in excellent condition and therefore a very desirable commemorative of George VI's 1937 coronation. Many commercial products were packaged in royal-souvenir containers.

WILLS'S CIGARETTES

WITH DISABLED EX-SERVICE MEN

WILLS'S CIGARETTES

AT WIMBLEDON

PLAYER'S CIGARETTES

HIS MAJESTY KING GEORGE VI

PLAYER'S CIGARETTES

H.M.'S BARGEMASTER
AND A WATERMAN

Given away singly in cigarette packs, cards like these are valued in complete sets. The two at top, from one set, show the future George VI at work and play. From another set are cards of him as king and of royal bargemen who marched in his coronation procession.

A loving cup made for Elizabeth's coronation is desirable because only 1,000 were made. This one is numbered 459 on the base.

In a model chair from Elizabeth II's investiture, a Scottish stone under the seat represents the Stone of Scone, symbol of rule over Scotland.

Valued as a collectible because none of its pieces have been lost, a jigsaw puzzle of Elizabeth's coronation procession bears a Victory trademark.

A souvenir book from Elizabeth's coronation, one inch square when closed, contains pictures of the new Queen and her husband, Prince Philip, as well as photographs of the throne and Westminster Abbey. Similar books from her 1977 Silver Jubilee are easier to find.

Cakes of soap were sold in great volume during jubilee celebrations, but apparently most have been used up. The same portrait was used on many other jubilee items, such as mugs, badges, record covers and perfume bottles.

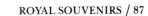

This laminated, cork-backed coaster shows Elizabeth II in her favorite diamond tiara. It is a common Silver Jubilee find.

Popular sayings —including one made familiar by the American television show Kojak, a favorite of the Queen's—encircle the traditional crown on an easy-to-find jubilee button.

COLLECTORS ORGANIZATIONS
Commemorative Collectors Society
25 Farndale Close
Long Eaton, NG10 3PA, United Kingdom

BOOKS
May, John and Jennifer, *Commemorative Pottery*

1780-1900. Charles Scribner's Sons, 1972.

Rodgers, David, *Coronation Souvenirs and Commemoratives.* Latimer New Dimensions Limited, 1975.

Warren, Geoffrey, *Royal Souvenirs.* Orbis Publishing Limited, 1977.

Samplers
Unique Needlework by Schoolgirls

Samplers are the only major collectible created by children. Not surprisingly, they have an innocent appeal and are a delight to look at, although samplers generally were school classroom assignments. Most were painstakingly stitched by schoolgirls between the 18th and the mid-19th Centuries to demonstrate their embroidery skills and mastery of the alphabet—the subjects that were generally considered important for girls at that time. This role in the education of young girls is one distinction that differentiates samplers from the somewhat similar mottoes *(page 98)*, signs that have been embroidered by adults since the mid-

---

Lewis Bunker Rohrbaugh is a securities analyst and genealogist who enjoys tracing the lineage of the makers of the samplers he collects.

19th Century with various sayings such as "What is home without Mother?"

Many of the verses that girls stitched onto their samplers were taken from poetry and such religious sources as *Divine and Moral Songs for Children.* Some of the inscriptions, however, show a certain amount of independence and seem to have come straight from the heart. One sampler that was worked in Pennsylvania around 1840 states, "This is mi needle work in the 14th year the affectionate daughter of Michael Mary Miller Sarah ann Miller is mi name." A Sheffield, Massachusetts, girl named Harriot Sacket inscribed a sampler to a friend: "preasant to. Polly Brass of Sheffiel d AUGUST 15 1795." Ruth Davis of Cumberland, New Jersey, in 1817 made it artlessly clear that her mother was dead. She inscribed her sampler: "This work I did to let you see What care my Papy took of me."

Statements such as these convey a feeling of intimacy that no other collectible can match. They also help to determine the worth of a sampler, for collectors especially value those that bear an original inscription and include the maker's name, a place or school name, and a date. Most prized are those that also have a colorful pictorial element—human figures, animals, trees and flowers, houses or Biblical scenes. Somewhat less desirable are signed and decorated samplers that include one or more alphabets, a row or two of numerals, and a verse. Least valuable are undated, anonymous examples that

have only a simple alphabet. A larger sampler usually brings more than a smaller one, although the rarest of all are probably the miniatures, which may be less than five inches square.

Since the mid-1970s the value of samplers has escalated dramatically. Yet lucky finds still. can be made. In 1978, for example, one collector found a small Quaker sampler dated 1801 *(page 92)* that she was able to buy for less than $100 because the dealer, who was misled by its austere design, underestimated its value. Samplers in less than perfect condition are not nearly so scarce—'nor are they so valuable. Serious collectors place great importance on condition and generally ignore samplers that are badly torn, faded, stained or mildewed. However, slight damage may have little effect on a sampler's charm or historical interest.

To check a sampler for fading, compare the color density of the front with that of the back, an easy task unless it is framed. An original frame, incidentally, adds to the value of a sampler and serves as evidence that the sampler is intact and untrimmed. If there is a frame, it should fit the sampler exactly and bear no signs of new saw marks or nail holes. Sometimes the framer's label will still be attached, providing a clue that may help in identifying a sampler's origin.

After design and condition, age is the principal influence on desirability. The oldest dated samplers were made in England in the 16th Century as pattern books in which adults assembled stitches and designs that they might later copy onto their linens. This custom began to die out with the proliferation of printed books of patterns, and the making of samplers gradually became an exercise for children.

By the 18th Century, samplers were being made in America at dame schools—informal establishments that were so named because they were run by women—and at such finishing schools as the one that was operated in the early 19th Century by the Widow Patten and her three daughters in Hartford, Connecticut. Mrs. Patten enrolled students not only from New England but from

A date and name clearly identify the 1830 sampler at right. The design of flowers, birds and trees at the bottom is unique to the Canterbury, New Hampshire, area and reflects the influence of one teacher.

Mary K Osgood's Sampler wrought in the
14th year of her age A D 1830 1234567890

Mary let virtue charm be thine
Charm that will increase and shine
They will cheer thy winter gloom
They will shine beyond thy tomb

Europe and the Caribbean as well—Bermuda, Jamaica, Trinidad, Barbados, Switzerland, England, France and Ireland. As she wrote in a letter to a friend: "Each young lady had a handsome framed piece on their return home, to present their parents, as embroidery was considered an indispensible accomplishment."

Very old samplers—those embroidered before the latter part of the 18th Century—are understandably so scarce as to be museum pieces. But a great many were done in the early decades of the 19th Century—before the Widow Patten's ideas about female education were superseded and samplers disappeared from the curricula of most schools. It is extremely hard to find samplers that were made after the 1850s.

The age of a sampler is often obvious in the date that the embroiderer stitched into the design. But in at least one case part of a date is missing because it was removed. The text that accompanies this example's Biblical scene reveals that Mary Hafline made the sampler in her 11th year; the date, however, is truncated to only three numerals: "178." Clearly, in her later years Mary removed the last figure from the date so that nobody could calculate her exact age.

When there is no stitched-in date, style can give a good indication of the period. During the centuries samplers were in fashion, vogues in shape and design came and went. The earliest American samplers, in imitation of English counterparts, were rather narrow, and their designs—examples of decorative borders and sometimes numbers, alphabets, names and dates—were arranged in very simple rows. By the mid-18th Century the samplers had broadened slightly in size and were less restricted in composition. Around the beginning of the 19th Century, the typical shape became more nearly square, a development that allowed additional space for verses and for illustrations of human figures, animals and buildings. Genealogical listings began to be incorporated on many samplers, and pictures of public buildings became popular design subjects. Overall, samplers of the 19th Century are more decorative than earlier ones and are dominated by their illustrations.

The illustrations provide clues that can help in identifying the origin even when no location is specified in the sampler itself. Although many teachers probably used published pictures as their inspiration for the compositions they wanted their students to depict, each teacher tended to sketch them in an individual way and also to add her own embellishments. The result was that a

This English sampler, very desirable because it is so old, was made in 1672 in the long and narrow form that was popular in Europe at that time; few in this shape were made in America. Beneath the alphabet at the top are intricate embroidery motifs that were worked in horizontal bands displaying a variety of stitches.

number of samplers overseen by one teacher may portray a similar scene.

A sampler with an illustration showing one or more black slaves serving white masters and mistresses and also depicting orange trees almost certainly is one made at the turn of the 19th Century in Newburyport, Massachusetts. Who the teacher was and why she favored this tropical fantasy are not known, but the same scene appears on at least three samplers that are traceable to that period and place.

Similarly, the depiction of grass and sky in green, white, and blue or gray thread sewed with unraveled, rippled silk in long stitches means that the sampler was most likely made by a student of Sarah Stivour, who ran a school in Salem, Massachusetts, from 1778 until 1786. There are 10 of these in existence. From Miss Polly Balch's school in Providence, Rhode Island, at least five samplers appeared between 1785 and 1810 that contain a depiction either of the old State House in Providence or of University Hall in that city.

Figuring out where, when and by whom a sampler was made is only the first stage of its identification, for detailed information about its background adds to its value. In many cases much of the history of the young embroiderer and her family can be learned. The three basic clues of name, date and place, which are likely to be stitched in, narrow the search, pointing to local libraries, historical and genealogical societies, churches and government offices that can be helpful. Such insti-

tutions are sources of documents that may cover the period involved and that in many cases can be linked by name to the sampler's maker. School records, for example, may list her name and note tuition payments; her home may be traced through real estate transactions on file in town and government offices.

My own experience in genealogy gives me an advantage in pursuing this kind of inquiry. In 1977 I bought a flower-embroidered sampler *(page 97)* that appealed to me both because of its style and because it had been made by a girl named Mehitable Bunker. I am a Bunker on my mother's side of the family. Some checking of family records revealed exactly what I had hoped to find: 12-year-old Mehitable was a distant cousin, a niece of my great-great-grandfather.

I like to believe that, whatever problems Cousin Mehitable faced with her stitching and however much work she had to undo and start over, the finished product gave her a great degree of pride. There is evidence that not every child who made a sampler enjoyed her work. Ten-year-old Patty Polk of Kent County, Maryland, for example, left no doubt about her feelings. The sampler she made about 1800 bluntly proclaims: "Patty Polk did this and she hated every stitch she did in it. She loves to read much more."

For related material, see the articles on Coverlets, Embroidery, Hooked Rugs, Lace, Needlework Tools, Quilts and Silk Pictures in separate volumes of this encyclopedia.

Anna Swett ran out of room for her letters and put the last "t" of her name on the line above —a detail that makes her sampler especially endearing.

Armenia Lyon's work portrays prized Biblical scenes, including Adam and Eve and the warriors Caleb and Joshua. Her sampler is very rare because it suggests the time it took to make: She started "her work aged 8 years in the year 1805 finished in 1806."

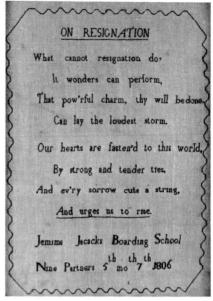

A sampler stitched on homespun (above), with no picture or identification, was probably made early in the 19th Century. The "U" and the "V" are out of order in the top two alphabets, correct in the bottom one.

A characteristically austere Quaker sampler, made in 1806 at the Nine Partners school in New York State, is desirable. Similar samplers with the same wavy border were made at another Quaker school in Pennsylvania.

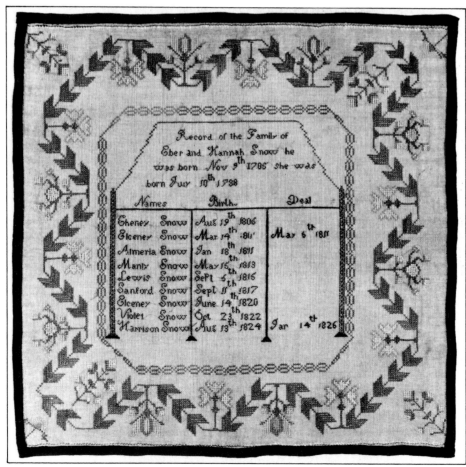

One of the most popular and prized types of samplers is the family register. Most listed the names of parents and children and included their birth and death dates. Eber and Hannah Snow named their seventh child after their second, who had died in 1811.

This unusual and desirable map sampler from England was stitched freehand with colored thread on silk. Most freehand samplers were done in black thread.

Samplers That Are Maps

Map samplers were in vogue in England in the late 18th Century, but they never became very popular in America. Fewer than 30 American map samplers, which probably are the work of older girls who were studying both geography and needlework, are known to survive. This small group includes some quite ambitious projects, one showing all of North and South America, for example, another essaying a map of the whole world. Most of the mapmakers, however, limited themselves to a country or region.

Some maps were made with commercial silk patterns; these are less interesting and less valuable than those worked freehand, usually on linen. The quality of needlework varies, but all map samplers are sought.

The sampler shown above displays many of the elements collectors prize: beautifully stitched alphabets and numerals, the name of the embroiderer, a date, and

unusually lavish decoration, which includes a vine, trees and flowers, a house, a windmill and eagles. One lack: Mary Rogers did not record where she made it.

Collectors look for samplers whose identifications include the name of the supervising teacher or the name of the school. Anna E. Tinkham not only recorded the fact that her needlework was accomplished "under the tuition of E. A. Hanks 1829" but also depicted schoolmistress Hanks, the schoolhouse and some of her fellow pupils. Although she did not name the school or the town, the sampler is believed to have been made in the Brattleboro area of Vermont, where the collector bought it at an auction in 1976.

A sampler by Mehitable Bunker, a forebear the collector traced through family records, has a well-designed and skillfully executed flower border, baskets of flowers and several alphabets, making it a good example of the elaborate work required of early-19th Century schoolgirls.

The design might have been predrawn on linen for the motto above, which incorporates the saying that is probably the most common of all.

Homely Sayings in Embroidery

Unlike samplers, created mainly as classroom exercises by schoolgirls, needlework mottoes are the work of hobbyists, usually adults. They became popular in the late 1800s and are still made. In place of alphabets, numbers and designs, mottoes have only a scene, usually domestic, and a saying.

Mottoes are less valuable than samplers, partly because they were made recently in large numbers. Most were stitched over preprinted patterns, not as individual creations. The more desirable are unusual in design, color or material, like the appliqués at left.

Worked about 1920, this motto is more valuable than most because appliqués were used for the utensils, tablecloth and shelf.

Like the motto at left, the example above was made around 1920 and is valued for its appliqué work — in this case, the cat.

On the tree of life eternal
Maid let all thy hope be staid

Which alone for ever vernal
Bears a leaf that shall not fade

Because wool thread, which cannot be worked as finely as silk, was used on this English sampler, the stitchery is below the level of most made in *that country. However, the colors have held up well, and value is further enhanced by inclusion of the names of the maker and her school.*

MUSEUMS

Cooper-Hewitt Museum
New York, New York 10028

Daughters of the American Revolution Museum
Washington, D.C. 20006

Henry Francis du Pont Winterthur Museum
Winterthur, Delaware 19735

The Metropolitan Museum of Art
New York, New York 10028

Museum of Fine Arts
Boston, Massachusetts 02115

Philadelphia Museum of Art
Philadelphia, Pennsylvania 19101

BOOKS

Bolton, Ethel Stanwood, and Eva Johnston Coe,
American Samplers. Peter Smith Publisher,
Inc., 1973.

Harbeson, Georgiana Brown, *American Needlework.*
Bonanza Books, 1967.

Krueger, Glee F.:
A Gallery of American Samplers: The Theodore H. Kapnek Collection. E. P. Dutton, 1978.
New England Samplers to 1840. Old Sturbridge Village, 1978.

Swan, Susan B., *Plain and Fancy, American Women and Their Needlework: 1700-1850.* Holt, Rinehart and Winston, 1977.

Science Fiction
Prophetic Fantasies of the Future

When French writer Jules Verne presented his grandson with the manuscript for *From the Earth to the Moon*, his 1865 novel describing a lunar orbit by a manned spacecraft, he said, "I know that you will see men go to the moon and you will be able to measure the accuracy of the images I created." Jean Jules-Verne did indeed see men go to the moon, and the details were much as his grandfather had predicted: The flight was American, there were three men aboard, the launch was made from Florida and the landing was made in the Pacific.

The prophecy in the writings of Verne and a host of others before and since is one of the fascinations

---

Gerry de la Ree, who lives in New Jersey, is a publisher of anthologies of science-fiction illustrations.

---

for collectors of the fantasies known as science fiction. The genre has attracted fans who speak a special language *(box, page 102)*. They assemble for conventions, or "cons"—an attendance of 5,000 was recorded at one "worldcon." At cons the fans sometimes bid at auction "Blochs" on a chunk of an author's time, for lunch or a conversation (tradition has it that the first writer to be thus auctioned was named Robert Bloch).

Although collectors acquire almost anything connected with the subject—magazines, original art work for books and magazines, and television and movie memorabilia—most concentrate on books. The prizes are first editions (see the article on Books in a separate volume of this encyclopedia).

The earliest science fiction is very old and so rare that first editions are museum pieces. The authors that fans of science fiction seek fall into three groups. First there are the 19th Century writers, led by Jules Verne. A second group consists of 20th Century authors who are famous for general works but who were responsible for some outstanding science fiction; Britain's Aldous Huxley is a prime example. A third group—the largest—is

This painting was created by Earle Bergey for Thrilling Wonder Stories, a science-fiction pulp magazine. In the chauvinist jargon of fans, it shows a BBB—a Big-Bosomed Babe—a specialty of the artist, who is equally noted for his portrayals of BEMs, or Bug-Eyed Monsters.

composed of 20th Century specialists in science fiction.

Most desirable of Verne's works are four of the early novels. The desirable editions are not the original French versions, but the first translations published in Britain and the United States: *From the Earth to the Moon* (Newark, New Jersey, 1869) and an edition containing this work plus the sequel, *From the Earth to the Moon, Direct in 97 Hours 20 Minutes: and a Trip Around It* (London, 1873; New York, 1874); *Journey to the Center of the Earth* (London, 1872; New York, 1874); and *Twenty Thousand Leagues under the Sea* (London, 1873; Boston, 1873).

Ranking in collectibility with Verne is H. G. Wells. Most prized is *The Time Machine*, his first novel, published in 1895 both in England and the United States. Two collectible contemporaries of Wells in England are George Griffith, whose best-known title, *The Angel of the Revolution,* was published in England in 1893, and M. P. Shiel, whose *Purple Cloud* and *Lord of the Sea* came out in England in 1901. Among the works of American writers, the 1914 book *Darkness and Dawn,* by George Allan England, has a collectible value about equal to that of the works of Griffith and Shiel.

In the second category, landmark science fiction by writers who were not science-fiction specialists, the most collectible titles are Aldous Huxley's *Brave New World* and George Orwell's *1984*. Huxley's book is notable for a number of reasons. It takes place in 632 A.F. (After Ford—that is, Henry Ford) and concerns genetic manipulation involving test-tube babies, a populace kept docile by a tranquilizing drug called "soma," and a love story involving a man named Marx and a woman named Lenina. First editions of the Huxley and Orwell books rank with the most desirable of the Wells titles.

The same ranking is enjoyed by only three titles by 20th Century writers: Frank Herbert's 1965 *Dune,* Ray Bradbury's 1950 *Martian Chronicles* and Olaf Stapledon's 1930 *Last and First Men.* Edgar Rice Burroughs, best known as the creator of Tarzan, is a special case. He wrote 11 novels set on Mars and four set on Venus. All are scarce, and first editions of the earliest—among them *A Princess of Mars*—can bring prices higher than any other 20th Century American work in the genre.

Most 20th Century science-fiction writers were graduates of a special branch of journalism—the pulps. These

*These 1939 and 1940 copies of a fanzine, or fan magazine, called
Futuria Fantasia are valued because they were edited by a then-obscure
writer named Ray Bradbury, who became a leading science-fiction author. The cover is by Hannes Bok, whose illustrations are very collectible.*

A GLOSSARY OF FANSPEAK

*Many collectibles have a specialized vocabulary developed for tech-
nical reasons. Science fiction has a rather sexist "fanspeak" that
was developed for no better reason than the fun of it. Some of the
more commonly used terms are defined below.*

ADZINE: A fanzine *(see below)* that runs advertisements for
collectors.

BBB: Big-Bosomed Babe, a staple character in space opera
(see below).

BEM: Bug-Eyed Monster.

CON: A convention of science-fiction fans and collectors.

CROGGLED: Astounded.

CRUDZINE: A shoddily produced fanzine.

EGOBOO: Ego boost, a rewarding experience.

EYETRACKS: A book that has been read is covered with these
and is no longer in mint condition.

FAN: A devotee of science fiction.

FANDOM: The world of fans.

FANSPEAK: The special language of fans.

FANZINE: A magazine edited and produced as a hobby by
amateurs for fandom subscribers.

FEN: The plural of "fan" in fanspeak. The standard form
for addressing a group of fen is "gentlefen."

JAM: A book complete with dust Jacket And in Mint
condition.

ORIGANTH: Original anthology, a collection of science fiction never before published.

PROZINE: A commercial science-fiction magazine, such as
Amazing Stories or *Astounding*.

PSD: Pretty Scientist's Daughter, often a BBB *(see above)*.

SF: Science fiction.

SPACE OPERA: By analogy with "soap opera" and "horse
opera," stories, movies, television or radio dramas about
space, written to a formula of adventure and action.

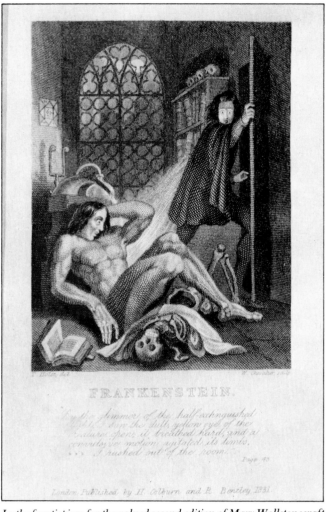

In the frontispiece for the valued second edition of Mary Wollstonecraft Shelley's Frankenstein, published in 1831, the monster comes to life as its creator flees. The first edition of 1818 is extremely rare.

A scientist who has reached the moon is watched by Selenites as he sends messages back to earth. This illustration is from H. G. Wells's 1901 novel, First Men in the Moon, *sought for both its subject and its author.*

cheaply printed magazines for mass audiences, named for their shoddy paper, are science-fiction collectibles second only to books. The first to be devoted to science fiction was *Amazing Stories,* founded in 1926 by a publisher and radio expert named Hugo Gernsback. The most desirable of the dozens that have appeared since *Amazing* came out is *Astounding Stories of Super-Science,* started in 1930 and renamed *Analog* in 1960 *(page 109)*.

Astounding's most famous editor was John W. Campbell Jr., who is especially remembered for insisting on scientific realism. One of his writers, Cleve Cartmill, got the magazine and himself in trouble during World War II by following this rule in a story, "Deadline," in which scientists of two warring nations sought to be the first to make an atomic bomb. Cartmill, who lived at a place named Manhattan Beach, knew nothing about the secret Manhattan Project, which then was creating an atomic bomb for the United States. He was considerably

puzzled when United States Army intelligence officers demanded the source of his fairly accurate description of the triggering method for the A-bomb.

Collectors looking for old magazines judge them partly by their illustrations. Among the most sought are issues containing pictures by Frank R. Paul *(page 107)* and Virgil Finlay *(page 106)*.

Much of this art work is so removed from any apparent reality that only a fan can understand it. But this is not true of movie posters. Of all such memorabilia, the rarest is a poster for *Metropolis,* a silent film of 1926 directed by Fritz Lang. Only two are known to exist. Easier to find, particularly at stores that specialize in such ephemera, are memorabilia from more recent movies.

For related material, see the articles on Books, Magazines, Movie Memorabilia and Posters in separate volumes of this encyclopedia.

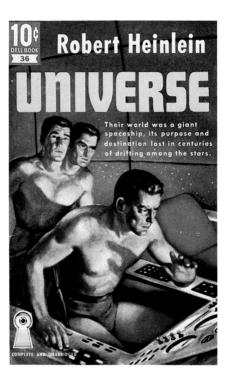

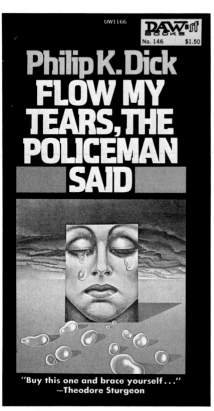

This 1943 paperback anthology is prized as a prototype. Beginning in the 1950s such anthologies largely replaced magazines as a major medium for science fiction.

A 10-cent paperback of Robert A. Heinlein's 1951 story is a rare volume by a much-collected author. Heinlein is best known for his works on space wars and colonization.

Above is the first paperback edition of a major work by a well-known writer. Collectors also prize it for the cover illustration by Hans Ulrich and Ute Osterwalder.

First editions of three futuristic narratives (above) were written by noted authors for a general audience but are prized as major works of science fiction. Orwell's 1984, first published in 1949, and Huxley's 1934 Brave New World are worth twice as much as Vonnegut's Player Piano, which appeared in 1952, because the first two authors are considered pioneers of the "dystopian," or antiutopian, novel.

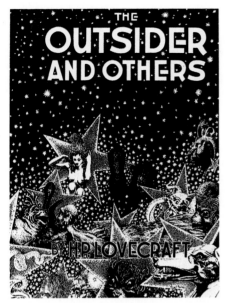

This 1939 collection of stories is valued for its author, who is a noted writer of science fiction, and for its rarity—it was first published in an edition of 1,268.

The dust jacket above includes one Bug-Eyed Monster described in the narrative by John W. Campbell Jr., who is remembered as an editor and guru to a generation of notable authors.

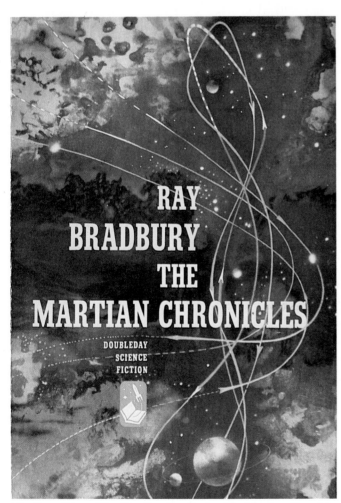

The first edition of Ray Bradbury's collection The Martian Chronicles appeared in 1950 and is considered highly desirable. It is one of the first books he published and is probably also his best-known work.

This 1953 novel about extraterrestrial intervention in earth's affairs is a sought-after first edition by the British author Arthur C. Clarke, known for his fiction, nonfiction and movie writing.

An illustration for C. L. Moore and Henry Kuttner's 1950 story "Earth's Last Citadel" depicts a group of alien invaders called Light-Wearers. The work is by Virgil Finlay, whose creations are sought after by science-fiction collectors.

The inhabitants of a planet flee as one of its suns begins to explode in this drawing by Frank R. Paul for a 1931 John Taine story in Won- *der Stories. Paul's work is especially desirable because he was a pioneer illustrator of science fiction.*

The premier issue of Amazing Stories in 1926 gave science fiction a magazine of its own for the first time by reprinting classic authors. It was edited and published by Hugo Gerns- back, who was probably the single most influential person in the development of science fiction. Hugos, the annual awards for achievement in the field, are named for him.

The most collectible science-fiction magazine is Astounding, edited by John W. Campbell Jr. for 34 years. During the periodical's long career as a monthly—the first issue is at upper right—it published nearly all the leading writers of the genre, including Isaac Asimov (above). It changed its subtitle several times and eventually its title (far right). A complete set, from the first issue in 1930 through 1977, brought $3,000 in 1979.

Anne Francis dances with a robot in a publicity photograph from the 1956 movie Forbidden Planet. Such stills are popular, easily found collectibles.

A 1977 issue of the movie cameramen's professional journal (above) is prized for its article explaining trick photography in the film Star Wars.

This poster was done for the 1953 film version of H. G. Wells's War of the Worlds. Posters are the most sought-after science-fiction movie collectibles.

A lobby card promotes the 1955 movie Invasion of the Body Snatchers. *These cards are not as desirable as other kinds of movie posters to science-fiction collectors, but Body Snatchers is considered a classic and anything connected with it is desirable.*

LIBRARIES
Dr. J. Lloyd Eaton Fantasy and Science Fiction
Collection
University of California
Riverside, California 92507

George Arents Research Library
Syracuse University
Syracuse, New York 13210

COLLECTORS ORGANIZATIONS
Los Angeles Science Fantasy Society (LASFS)
11513 Burbank Boulevard
North Hollywood, California 91601

New England Science Fiction Association (NESFA)
Box G, MIT Branch Post Office
Cambridge, Massachusetts 02139

PERIODICALS
Locus, Locus Publications, San Francisco, California
94119

BOOKS
Ash, Brian, ed., *The Visual Encyclopedia of Science
Fiction.* Harmony Books, 1977.

Nicholls, Peter, *The Science Fiction Encyclopedia.*
Doubleday and Company, Inc., 1979.

Scrimshaw
Legacies from the Days of Whaling

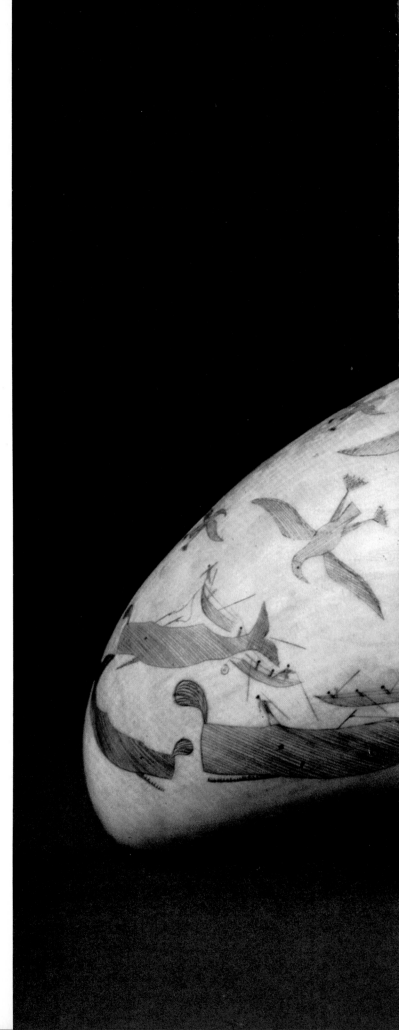

Even as recently as the 1960s, says one well-known collector of the whalemen's carvings called scrimshaw, "yard sales were the major place I found scrimshaw, or some farmer cleaning out his junk. If you kept your eyes open, you could find some." Hardly more than a decade later, beautiful pieces that had been picked up for $25 were bringing $1,000 or more at auction. In 1970 a physician who collected scrimshaw as

Barbara Johnson, who acquired her first piece of scrimshaw in 1967, proceeded to assemble one of the largest collections in the country.

well as readily identifiable antiques reported a burglary of his office; the burglars ignored his antiques but cleaned out his scrimshaw.

This transformation of 19th Century souvenirs into 20th Century treasure owes less to the current vogue for collecting than it does to one particular collector: President John F. Kennedy, who kept scrimshaw in view on his desk. Kennedy's collecting agent, George D. Wintress, recalled in a conversation with a reporter, "You people in the newsmagazines created the scrimshaw boom by publishing full-color photographs of the Oval Office desk. I had to advise the President to stop giving pieces away. With each new bit of publicity the market got tighter and tighter."

The unusual folk art that now intrigues so many people developed during the rich days of American whaling because the sailors had lots of spare time—a voyage might last years, and exciting chases of the quarry were brief, separated by long stretches of fruitless cruising. Sunday was a holy day, reserved by many captains for rest and prayer. "According to rules, we abstain from all labor on Sunday," wrote one sailor in his diary. "A few men write or draw; some scrimshone, or carve keep-

An extremely valuable piece of scrimshaw (right) provides a wealth of whale-hunting detail on the surface of a tooth eight inches long and four inches at its widest point. Sea gulls wheel overhead as four whaleboats approach five whales. At the left, one whale shatters a boat with its tail. On the whaler, a sailor atop the mainmast signals the boats by flag.

sakes for friends from bone of the whale's jaw, the ivory of the teeth, or the rich woods and mother-of-pearl found on the islands."

Most of the objects on which the whalemen lavished loving care were made for women waiting for them, they hoped, back home. From strips of baleen, the horn-like substance in the mouth of some species of whales, they made busks decorated with sentimental scenes and sayings and designed to stiffen corsets. They made rings, bracelets, knitting needles, picture frames, baskets, jagging wheels to crimp the edge of pies, butter spreaders, spool racks, needlecases, necklaces, swifts on which to wind yarn, earrings, charms, thimbles and folding fans. For children they fashioned dolls and other toys. For themselves they made ditty boxes for storage and a variety of shipboard tools such as mallets, fids for loosening knots in rope, belaying pins, tool handles and cleats. And they engraved teeth with pictures: pretty women, happy domestic scenes and, most valuable of all, stirring views of the whaling life such as whalers standing out to sea, whaleboats in hot pursuit and boats being stove in by whales.

A decorated tooth is especially desirable if it bears the name of a whaling vessel—one such tooth sold in 1979 for $29,500. The most famous teeth are those marked with the name of the whaler *Susan* out of Nantucket and with the name of the whaleman who carved them, Frederick Myrick. They come from voyages made in the 1820s and are among the earliest known.

Not all scrimshaw, however, is so rare and valuable. Small items, particularly those made for utilitarian purposes and left largely undecorated, come up for sale at prices that, while not low, are relatively affordable. Many are simple tools and other items sailors used aboard ship *(pages 116-117)*. Others are household objects such as various knitting and sewing aids *(page 121)*.

There also are rare small pieces of scrimshaw that are valued for their associations but are the subject of controversy. One is a piece of ivory, bone or wood two or three inches long. Most collectors, including myself, believe it a bodkin; others consider it a harpooner's peg, through which harpoon line was paid out as the whale sought to escape. Another much argued small piece— possibly of recent origin—is the mortgage token, a disk inscribed to mark the date on which a home mortgage was finally paid up. The tokens were set into the top of the newel post on the stairs.

There is such a variety of scrimshaw because the word (spelled many different ways) came to mean anything made by off-duty whalemen aboard ship. The makers— called scrimshanders—used whatever materials came to hand. This obviously included whale teeth, bone and baleen. It also included materials picked up on shore trips—sandalwood, rosewood, ebony, satinwood, ma-

A pair of engraved teeth shows a family at leisure in a garden (left) and children with toy sailboats. A pair of matched teeth like this is worth considerably more than the two would be separately.

hogany, teak, camphorwood and gumwood as well as common American woods, coconuts, tortoise shells and mother-of-pearl—and metals such as silver, copper and brass. When nonwhale materials were used, they were usually combined with whale ivory or bone; many picture frames, for example, were fashioned of walnut or mahogany with whale-ivory or mother-of-pearl inlay.

The most desirable scrimshaw now can be found mainly at specialized auctions, such as those held on Cape Cod and in the large galleries of New York City. But good pieces still turn up in unusual places. I obtained a tooth carved by Frederick Myrick of the *Susan* from a builder I know in New England; he found it in an old house he was remodeling. Old houses that have stayed in one family for a long time are promising sources. I once was led to a valuable find by a phone call from a hometown neighbor, telling me about trunks found in the attic of what had been a whaling family's house; the trunks contained a cache of scrimshaw that had been stored for nearly 100 years.

Collectors should look beyond the obvious Massachusetts whaling centers of New Bedford and Nantucket

A Plague of Fakery

Scrimshaw has become so popular since the 1960s that many pieces that look like whalemen's carvings—by some estimates, more than half of those offered for sale—are the work of artists who never saw the sea, let alone a whale. Much of this modern work is done, with no intent to deceive, by carvers supplying the market for *objets d'art.* But some is intentionally faked, and spotting the fakes is difficult.

Most of the modern pieces are engraved teeth, since they are the most avidly sought scrimshaw. Simple forms such as fids, bodkins and clothespins are less likely to be forgeries—because authentic scrimshaw of this type is more common than teeth. The designs also offer clues to authenticity. The old scrimshanders knew their subjects intimately, and they made faithfully detailed pictures of ships. Inaccuracies or anachronisms are telltale signs of recent work. And if a design incorporates astrological symbols or mushrooms, you can be almost certain no whaleman made it.

With experience, you can judge age from materials. Whale ivory and bone have a distinctive grain. Much authentic scrimshaw is buff-colored, because whalemen polished each piece with oil that darkened it; handling would darken it further. But new pieces can be darkened with motor oil, coffee or tea, so a dark piece should be examined for crevices and unfinished areas common in modern pieces. A colored piece should be faded. Incisions in an engraved piece should be shallow—whalers worked with relatively crude tools, not the thin sharp knives of today.

Typical of the fine modern engraving on ivory is this tooth by Clyde King. The style—particularly the head-on, foreshortened view of the ship—clearly distinguishes it from 19th Century scrimshaw.

Obvious inaccuracies mark this tooth as fake. The whale seems an unlikely cross between a sperm whale and a right whale, and the whalemen are dressed inappropriately. Worse, the harpooner is in the wrong place in the whaleboat—he normally knelt at the bow.

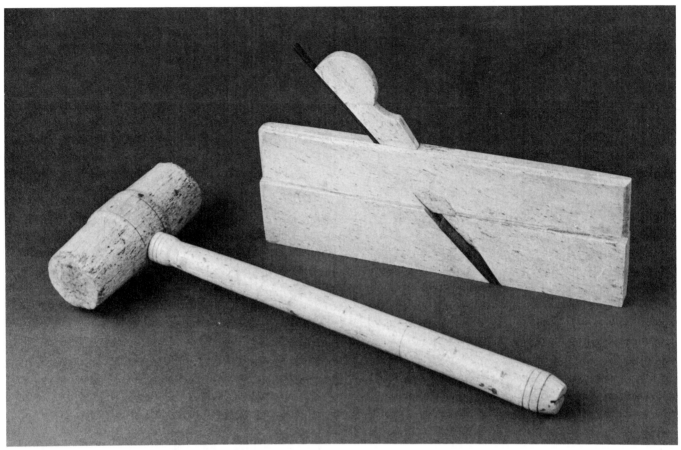

Two tools for shipboard use are a mallet and a plane for making decorative moldings. Both are made of bone, the plane having a steel blade.

Tools like these are considerably easier to find than scrimshaw that has been fancifully shaped and decorated for gifts.

and keep in mind San Francisco and the whaling ports of Long Island, such as Sag Harbor and Southampton. Scrimshaw can also be found far from the sea. Much ended up in the Midwest, since many New England whalemen retired to farm what was once the Western Reserve, now part of Ohio, and brought their tools and mementos with them. One collector got a fine piece in Aspen, Colorado. And I found scrimshaw in South America while browsing through a pawnshop in Chile.

An experienced collector follows hunches. One man, spotting a candlestick that the owner thought "just an old bone," noticed a hint of design under the layers of dirt. He bought the candlestick for only a few dollars, cleaned it and found, underneath all the dust, beautifully carved scrimshaw.

When looking for scrimshaw, a collector must guard against fakes. Ivory is being carved today, and some is passed off as 19th Century scrimshaw *(page 115)*. Few carvings were made by whalemen after the 19th Century because the industry declined so dramatically then. A fleet that had numbered 735 in 1846 was reduced to six by 1912—the result of disaster, changes in commerce, and the near-extinction of the whale.

The whale is now protected in the United States by the Endangered Species Act, which restricts commercial sales and interstate commerce. However, it is not the law that hampers the collector but the limited supply of authentic pieces. Still, some experts believe that quantities of old scrimshaw pieces are waiting to be found.

One farfetched tale that inspires the search describes a set of more than 50 pieces unusually rich in human interest. They were said to be the work of James Taylor, an unusually well educated Englishman who in the 1870s undertook to make for his beloved Elizabeth Royston 52 busks—presumably one for each week of the year. Twelve were illustrated with Shakespearean scenes, each from a different play. Others drew on the *Iliad.* Unfortunately, when Taylor came to deliver the last lot of six, he discovered Mrs. Royston with a gentleman. Using a busk as a weapon, he belabored first the man and then the widow. Taylor went to jail for assault, and Elizabeth Royston sold 52 busks to an art dealer. Not one has been found—so far.

For related material, see the articles on Canes, Folk Art and Nautical Gear in separate volumes of this encyclopedia.

The bowl of this dipper is a coconut shell, the handle is mahogany. Ivory is used for ornamental fittings, and a brass ring for a hanger.

Baleen, which comes from the mouths of some species of whale, was steamed and bent to make this ditty box, a container used aboard ship to store a sailor's sewing and mending gear. The rivets are made of pewter.

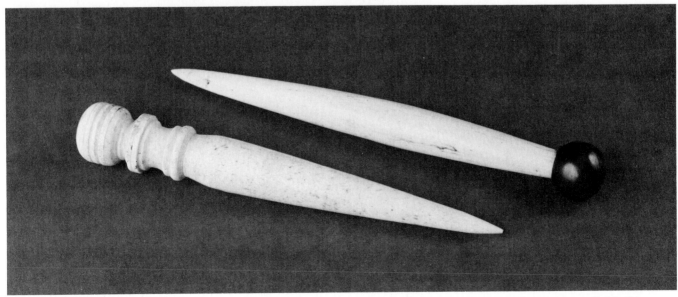

These two fids are both of whalebone, but the one at top is fitted with a wooden knob. Fids were used by sailors to loosen knots in rope and to separate strands for splicing. Smaller versions, called bodkins, were made by the scrimshanders for their womenfolk's needlework.

A catch-ball toy, five inches long (above), was originally made of whale ivory, but the tip was later repaired with a piece of bone and the string is a recent replacement. Relatively few scrimshaw toys are found, and they are correspondingly valuable.

This miniature stand of mahogany and ivory may have been made to display a locket. The portrait—of a Martha's Vineyard whaling captain—was added by the collector.

Two busks (above), used for stiffening corsets, are lavishly engraved. The one at left bears (from top) a heart, the Lord's Prayer, a girl and the inscription "Yes, I will leave my father's halls," the same girl and geometric designs. The busk at right has a rose, a sun, a flowering bush, a star and a bird.

The rolling pins above are in the simple style known as Nantucket. The one at top is made of beechwood and walrus ivory; the other is made completely of bone.

This vessel, three inches tall, is a single carved piece of ivory resting on tortoise shell. It may have been an open saltcellar.

Decorated with red and black ink, a complete place setting for a doll is made of whale ivory. The set is unusual and valuable.

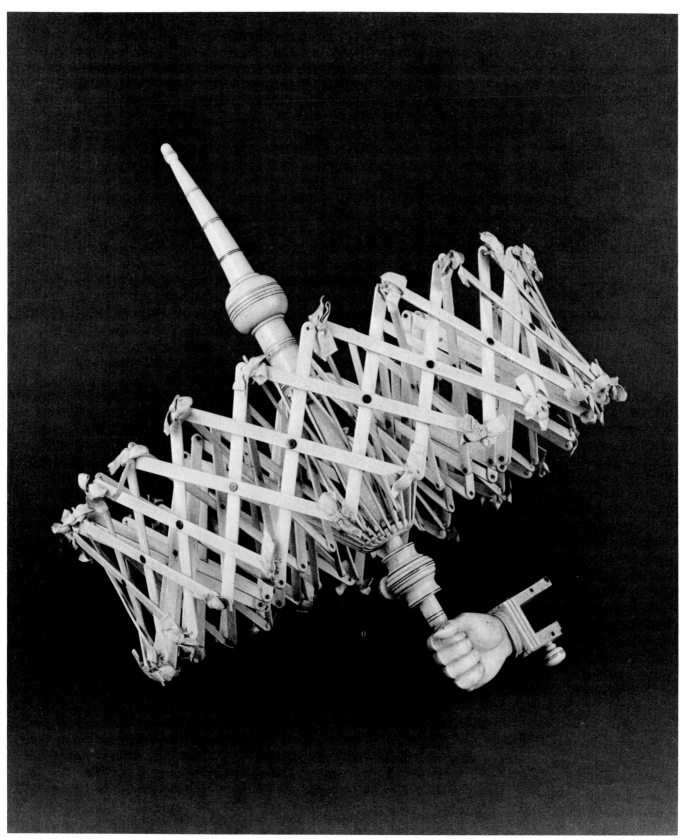

Making a swift, or yarn winder, like this one of whale ivory and bone with ribbons, was considered the ultimate test of a whaleman's scrim- *shawing skills. The clamp to the right of the carved hand fastened to the edge of a table while the swift was being used.*

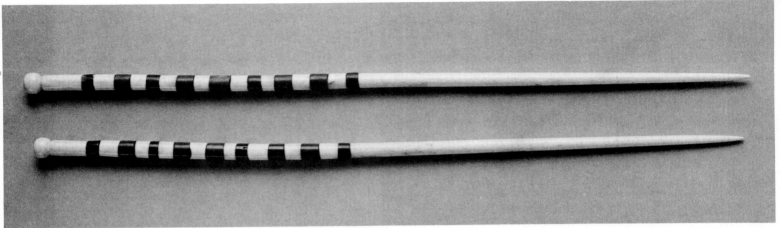

These scrimshaw knitting needles combine points made of bone with handles made of ivory alternating with light and dark mahoganies, the whole strung together on what probably are thin metal rods. Such knitting needles are valued by collectors.

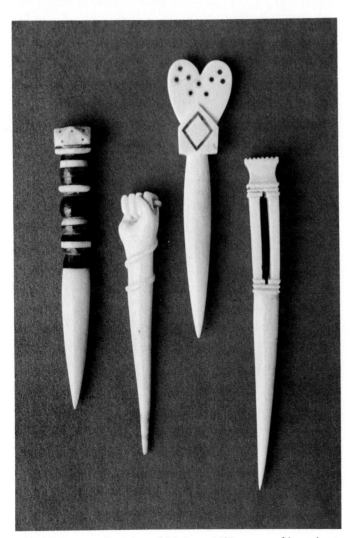

These bodkins, small versions of fids (page 117), were used in sewing to make holes in fabric. The one at the left is ivory, wood and silver. The combination of fist and snake that makes up the handle of the one second from left is a common scrimshaw motif.

MUSEUMS
The Kendall Whaling Museum
Sharon, Massachusetts 02067

Mystic Seaport
Mystic, Connecticut 06355

Nantucket Whaling Museum
Nantucket, Massachusetts 02554

The National Maritime Museum
San Francisco, California 94109

New Bedford Whaling Museum
New Bedford, Massachusetts 02740

The Peabody Museum
Salem, Massachusetts 01970

Sag Harbor Whaling Museum
Sag Harbor, New York 11963

The Whaling Museum Society
Cold Spring Harbor, New York 11724

BOOKS
Ashley, Clifford W., *The Yankee Whaler.* Houghton Mifflin Co., 1926.

Barnes, Clare, Jr., *John F. Kennedy, Scrimshaw Collector.* Little, Brown & Co., 1969.

Flayderman, E. Norman, *Scrimshaw and Scrimshanders: Whales and Whalemen.* N. Flayderman and Company, Inc., 1972.

Frere-Cook, Gervis, ed., *The Decorative Arts of the Mariner.* Little, Brown & Co., 1966.

Stackpole, Edouard A., *Scrimshaw at Mystic Seaport.* The Marine Historical Association, Inc., 1958.

Shaker Crafts
Furnishings Fit for Angels

The priest-poet Thomas Merton once wrote that Shaker chairs have a unique grace because they were made by people capable of believing angels might come and sit in them. We responded to that grace without knowing anything about the Shakers or their beliefs when, at an auction in 1950, a simple pair of ladder-back rockers caught our eyes. We bought them for $16 each, thinking we had found two exceptionally well made pieces of country furniture. A friend said they were Shaker chairs and told us something of the Shakers' history. We were intrigued. Despite assurances from several dealers that there was no Shaker furniture

Richard and Elizabeth Wells are retired schoolteachers who live in an old New England farmhouse furnished almost entirely with Shaker-made pieces they have collected since the 1950s.

left to collect, we now have a houseful of pieces by these peerless craftsmen of the 19th and early 20th Centuries.

The Shakers were an American fundamentalist sect, formally referred to as the United Society of Believers in Christ's Second Appearing, that withdrew from the world's "great and wicked cities" in the late 18th Century to build a heaven on earth in self-contained communities. Known derisively as the "Shaking Quakers" because of the ecstatic devotions they conducted to "shake out sin," they practiced celibacy and communal ownership of all property. By the 1850s the movement had swelled to 6,000 brothers, sisters and adopted children living in 19 communities from Maine to Kentucky. A little more than a century later only two Shaker communities were still in operation and there were fewer than 10 members left, all of them elderly women living at the settlements in Sabbathday Lake, Maine, and Canterbury, New Hampshire; a few other communities are preserved as museums.

The Shakers' values survive in the products of their hands. They made almost everything their communities

A child's-size sewing desk and the spinning top resting on it were produced by Shaker craftsmen for use only within the community, and both are exceedingly rare. The bentwood rocker, also sized for a child, is in a Shaker style made only in the late 19th and early 20th Centuries; produced to be sold to the outside world, it is less rare than the desk.

needed and they sold things to the "world" to pay for raw materials and for what they could not produce themselves. The organization and care for quality they brought to their commercial enterprises made them popular with customers, and their beautiful, simple chairs, in particular, were produced in quantity. The elegantly severe style of their pieces makes them easily recognizable. The style is remarkably uniform, despite minor variations introduced by individual communities, because Shaker leaders in the Watervliet, New York, settlement promulgated and supervised standard designs.

Collectors of Shaker crafts look for both their commercial products and the things they made for their own use. Their furniture, world-famous for its beauty and simplicity, its practicality and meticulous craftsmanship, is the most desirable. But collectors also seek kitchen equipment, shop tools, containers, cleaning equipment and pegboards—the rows of multipurpose pegs that ran around the walls of every Shaker room (*page 128*). For example, a small wooden garden-seed box with the inner and outer labels intact is worth about the same as an armchair or a rocker; with only the outer label it is worth half as much. Also rare, but not in great demand, are the hooded cloaks that Shakers made for women. Single oval wooden boxes are quite expensive and sets of nested oval boxes are hard to find and very valuable.

The Shakers' own furnishings are the most valuable partly because quantity is so limited. Among the small items most frequently found are hanging shelves and small hanging cupboards like the one on page 129. Occasional furniture—small tables, washstands and candlestands—is very desirable, but the most valuable of all are large dining tables. Chairs for specific uses, such as dining chairs and chairs for weavers and ironers, are also rare. Much more accessible are chairs made for the world. Rockers and side chairs are the easiest to come by, worth about half as much as armchairs.

Among the more available Shaker collectibles are bottles in which such cures as Mother Siegel's syrup were purveyed. Paper items—the almanacs in which they advertised their medicines and the postcards they sold to tourists around the turn of the century—also are fairly easy to find.

Knowing about the Shakers' way of life can be helpful

in identifying their furniture; their beliefs, centered on simplicity, order and utility, directed their craftsmanship. Their rules of conduct, derived from inspirations they called gifts of God, fanatically sought to impose order on their lives, overlooking no daily act: "It is contrary to order to put the left boot or shoe on first"; "It is contrary to order to put the left foot on the stairs first when ascending."

Shaker furniture translated this need for order into practicality, expressed in distinctive features. Their sewing desks—small chests, often with a pull-out shelf or drop leaf—were sometimes made with drawers on two sides so two Shaker sisters could work at once. Their beds and many of their counters roll on wooden casters. Some dining chairs have short backs so they can be pushed completely out of the way under the table; chairs for weavers have long legs and seats that tip slightly forward to make it easier to work the looms. Mirrors and sconces can be hung on pegs. One rocking chair has a drawer conveniently built in under the seat.

In some cases, conscientious attention to construction details led to unique designs. The Shakers' oval wooden boxes *(page 130)*, one of the most popular collectibles, have strong and distinctive "swallowtail" joints. Shaker dwelling houses led to designs that aid recognition of Shaker items. The sect's founder, Mother Ann Lee, said, "Clean your room well; for good spirits will not live where there is dirt. There is no dirt in heaven." To combat dirt, the Shakers invented the flat broom and adapted their furniture to facilitate the cleaning of the rooms. Their chairs were made to be light in weight so that when not in use they could be hung up on the walls on pegs, out of the way of cleaners' brooms. Thus the weight of a chair is evidence of its origin. Shaker chairs were made from exceptionally well cured wood, and nearly all originals are lighter than reproductions—to get a feeling for the weight of an original, heft one.

Shaker rules decreed that "fancy articles of any kind, or articles which are superfluously finished, trimmed or ornamented, are not suitable for Believers," that "Believers may not in any case, manufacture for sale, any article or articles which are superfluously wrought, and which would have the tendency to feed the pride and vanity of man," and that "beauty rests on utility." Such commandments required absolutely plain furnishings. Thus, furniture dressed up with veneers, ornamental carving or fancy painting is unlikely to be Shaker-made, while furniture finished with plain varnish or a thin stain of yellow, red, green or blue could very well be of Shaker origin.

Evidence of a single-minded dedication to the utmost in utility and fine craftsmanship is one indication that furniture might have been made by Shakers. In furniture made for their own use, the conclusive proof of origin is the individual maker's mark or a name that can be traced through Shaker membership records. Marked pieces are rare because the Shakers, believing that anonymity would discourage pride, forbade craftsmen to mark their work. A few did, however.

On 19th Century pieces, collectors may also find two-digit numbers that indicate the year when they were made, or a number-letter combination—G7, for example—identifying the room, shop or cabinet for which a piece was made. Since property was communal, the Shakers originally had rules against the use of marks to indicate personal ownership, but rules were relaxed as membership declined, and some small items, such as oval boxes and coat hangers *(page 126)*, were marked with users' initials in the late 19th Century. These are highly desirable.

The rules against identification did not apply to objects made for commercial sale; most were marked. A supporter remarked in the monthly Shaker newspaper that every time they began selling a product they were immediately confronted with counterfeits in the market that "looked like their goods before being used, but came to an end of their usefulness much sooner." That was especially true of their chairs. To protect themselves the Shakers registered a trademark in 1873 and applied decals *(page 134)* to their chairs, usually on a leg or the back of a slat. They also provided instructions for washing off the decal, but chairs retaining the original labels are fairly common.

The Shakers had been selling chairs from their communities almost from the time they first organized in 1787, but it remained for Brother Robert Wagan of the New Lebanon, New York, community to bring the industry to prominence in the 1860s. He organized mail-order catalogue sales, handled consignments to large cities in the East and Midwest, and eventually began supplying chairs to such large department stores as Marshall Field of Chicago.

All commercial Shaker chairs came in eight standard sizes, numbered 0 to 7 in order of increasing size; these size numbers, pressed into the back of the top slat, are still visible on chairs today. Most seats were either made of strips of woven worsted tape (offered in 14 colors) or fitted with wool-plush cushions, also manufactured by the Shakers. Tape seats often are found in deteriorated condition but they are easy to replace with commercially available tape. Early Shaker chairs with original rush, cane or wood-splint seats are rare because they were not mass-produced. So are chairs equipped with tilters *(page 136)*, which allow sitters to lean back in them; they were made for use only in the community.

Just as imitations of Shaker chairs were made in the 19th Century, so have reproductions been widely manufactured in the 20th Century, particularly during the

Elder Charles Greaves, wearing his Shaker garb and carrying his carpenter's tools, is pictured on one of a set of postcards sold to visitors at the Mount Lebanon, New York, community around the turn of the century. Similar postcards are easy to find.

The Shakers produced almanacs such as this one for sale and incidentally to advertise their flourishing business in herbal medicine. The mystery that was explained in the 1886 edition (left) concerned the preparation of their best-selling Mother Siegel's syrup. Shaker almanacs are desirable collectibles.

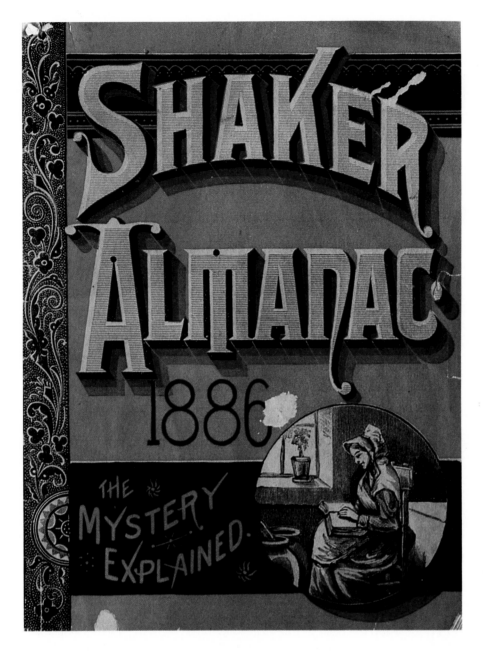

boom in Shaker collectibles that began in the 1950s. Most reproductions are marked as such, but some may be mistaken for or intentionally passed off as authentic.

Authentic chairs have a patina of age that cannot be reproduced. Many were made with mixed woods, such as the combination of walnut and maple on page 134, and reproductions are not; a chair made with a single kind of wood is not necessarily a reproduction, but one with mixed woods is very likely to be an original Shaker. Reproductions are not a problem in the case of bentwood rockers, such as our child's rocker *(page 122)*. These were made by the Shakers around the turn of the century, when their chair industry was coming to an end. Because the style is a deviation from the traditional Shaker form, they are not well known or reproduced. But they are available and should be watched for.

We were able to buy the small rocker on page 122 for only five dollars because it was hidden under a thick layer of added upholstery and the seller did not know what it was. Its market value now is many times what we paid.

If you ask a dealer how to collect Shaker crafts, you will probably hear what we were told half a lifetime ago—that none are available at reasonable prices. It is true that Shaker furniture has become much more popular and much higher in price, but we would still ignore the advice today as we did then. Bargains in the sense of great value for little money may be hard or impossible to find, but gratifying discoveries are not. Look for small estate sales in the areas of New York, Maine, New Hampshire, Massachusetts, Connecticut, Ohio and Kentucky where Shaker craftsmen worked. You may find a chair that is fit for an angel to sit in because it was made by a craftsman heeding Mother Ann's dictum, "Put your hands to work and your hearts to God."

The invention of clothespins, both plain and spring type, is credited by some authorities to Shakers. These examples came from the community at North Union, Ohio, but similar pins were produced by non-Shakers, and Shaker originals are difficult to authenticate.

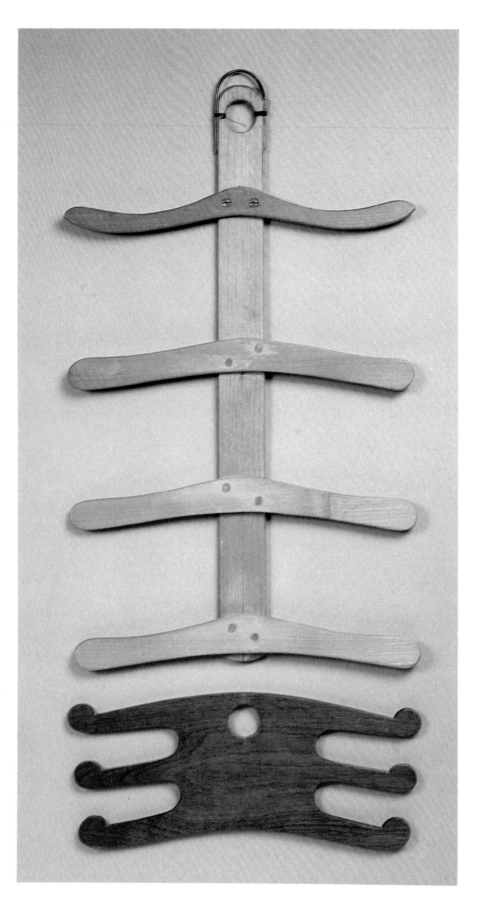

Multiple hangers for clothes were a Shaker spacesaver—and are relatively easy to find. The holes in the tops of these hangers allowed them to be hung from pegboards, the rails of pegs built into the walls of Shaker rooms.

Brooms, whisks and dusters of Shaker origin are desirable if they can be authenticated. The curved whisk was for clothes, and the whisk at bottom right was made to sprinkle ironing or to clean pots. A regular whisk is next to the wool duster at left.

The rare spinning wheel above bears the initials of David Meacham, a trustee at the New Lebanon Shaker community, where it was made. The

Shakers made their own textiles for clothes, bedding, woven chair seats and other uses. Women's cloaks are particularly collectible.

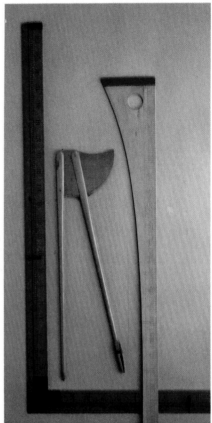

Shaker measuring tools are desirable. From left are a square, a compass, and a tailor's yardstick that was used to measure along the curve of a shoulder or thigh.

This Shaker tool cupboard was put together like a fine cabinet. Such small cupboards are among the more accessible pieces of the Shakers' own furniture. Also collectible are the tools in the cabinet. Difficult to tell apart from other craftsmen's tools of the same period, the ones made by the Shakers often have fine cherry or maple handles, and many are marked with a scribe line around the handle—the minimal Shaker concession to decoration.

Sides and lids of oval boxes are wooden strips joined at their ends by overlapping "fingers." Boxes are among the most popular Shaker collectibles.

Except for the rug, the vase on the table and the curtains, everything in this room in the authors' home was made by Shakers. The table is a rare tilt-top; the large counter might have been used in a workshop or large kitchen. The implements on the counter and on the hanging shelf above it are known to have come from Shaker communities; the framed picture is an advertisement for Shaker-grown seeds.

A tall, narrow cupboard in dark-stained pine contains two shelves behind the door and two drawers below it. The molding at the top and bottom is in a style unique to the Shaker community in Water- *vliet, New York. The stepstool to the left of the cupboard was a common item in Shaker dormitories and workshops, many of which had high shelves and drawers for neat, out-of-the-way storage.*

Used for sorting garden seeds, a two-drawer pine worktable has a rimmed top to keep the seeds from falling off; a slot at the front of the rim, visible at the right, made it easy to slide selected seeds off the table. Growing seeds for sale was a Shaker specialty.

Two features of a cherry candlestand are unmistakably Shaker: simple snake legs curving to the floor, and a plain tapered pedestal. Such tables are among the most sought after of Shaker furniture.

A washstand of tiger maple is evidence of the Shakers' willingness to use the finest woods for the most utilitarian function. Even a small piece of Shaker furniture like this is very valuable.

The Shaker armchair at right can be identified as made for general sale by a size number (not visible) on the back of the top slat. After 1873 the Shakers used a removable decal (above) to mark commercial chairs and footstools.

A mixture of woods was common in many Shaker chairs of the late 1800s. In this case walnut was used for the frame and maple for the rungs. The seat of woven tape and the tapered front legs are Shaker hallmarks.

Rocking chairs with arms were the Shakers' most popular model with their outside customers and are the most popular with 20th Century collectors. This one, with a seat 22 inches wide, is a No. 7, the largest built. The top rail, unique to Shaker chairs, was used to suspend a cushion, though it is called a shawl rail.

The Shakers' Special Touches

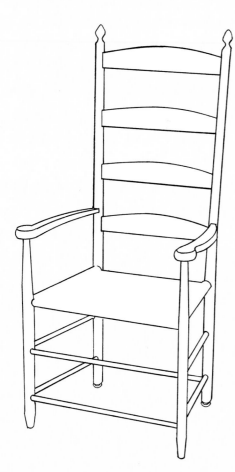

With the exception of tilters for chairs *(below, right)*, Shaker furniture construction was not unique. But the Shakers strove for excellence in the application of standard methods. They took great pains, and they routinely used very fine cabinetry techniques such as dovetailing *(opposite, bottom left)*. And, because they believed in honest simplicity, they often left construction details exposed rather than hiding them as other woodworkers customarily did.

The design and construction visible in the pieces illustrated on these pages can help identify Shaker furniture. Their presence is not in itself proof; however, the presence of all such features that are applicable to the piece supports evidence of style in confirming Shaker origin. And if none of these techniques can be recognized in a piece, it probably is not Shaker.

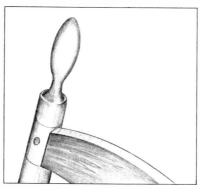

Shaker chairs—the type at left is a favorite collectible—generally have backs made of slats with beveled edges (above). The scribe marks on the side posts help position the slat for a pegged mortise joint.

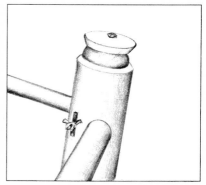

Tilters, introduced by the Shakers, are hemispherical feet (above). Tied to cups by thongs in the legs, they swivel to stay flat on the floor when the chair is tipped back. A thong can be seen in a slot in the leg.

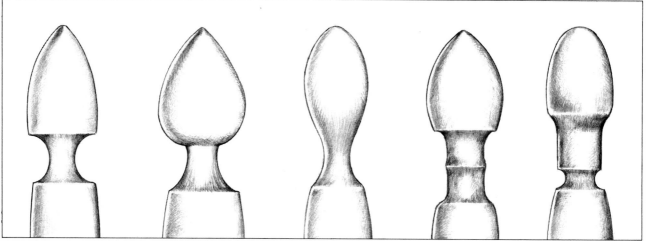

Five of the characteristic finials that Shakers fashioned on the side posts of their chair backs are sketched above. At far left is the shape adopted for commercial chairs. The one at center was used on chairs made by Shakers in the Canterbury, New Hampshire, community. All of the others appear on chairs made in New Lebanon, New York, Watervliet, New York, and Hancock, Massachusetts.

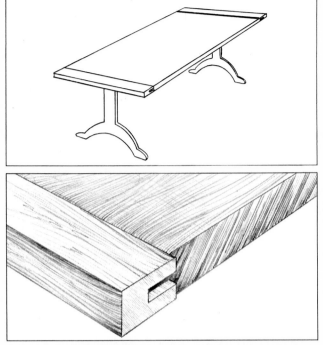

To prevent warping of a plank-top table (top), narrow boards, their grain at right angles to the plank grain, were fitted across the plank ends. Such tables are said to have breadboard ends. Breadboard ends extend beyond the table sides (bottom).

For added strength, even in a light-duty door like that of a cupboard (inset), a mortise-and-tenon, or tongue, joint was made with a rail tenon that extended clear through the stile mortise. To make the joint still stronger, angled pegs pinned tenon to mortise.

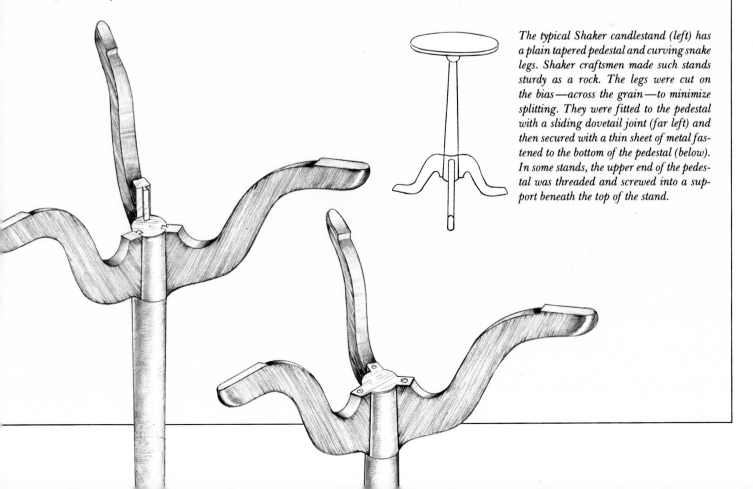

The typical Shaker candlestand (left) has a plain tapered pedestal and curving snake legs. Shaker craftsmen made such stands sturdy as a rock. The legs were cut on the bias—across the grain—to minimize splitting. They were fitted to the pedestal with a sliding dovetail joint (far left) and then secured with a thin sheet of metal fastened to the bottom of the pedestal (below). In some stands, the upper end of the pedestal was threaded and screwed into a support beneath the top of the stand.

Dominating a roomful of Shaker furniture, the cherry dining table—with typical breadboard ends—was used by Shaker elders and eldresses, who ate apart from their fellows. The other pieces include a 20-drawer apothecary chest (far left), a cheese press (partially obscured, in front of

the glass doors at left), a dry sink in the corner, and two large counters.
On the counter near the window are a candleholder and a spice chest.

MUSEUMS
Fruitlands Museum
Harvard, Massachusetts 01451

Hancock Shaker Community, Inc.
Pittsfield, Massachusetts 01201

Henry Francis du Pont Winterthur Museum
Winterthur, Delaware 19735

Milwaukee Art Center: Villa Terrace
Milwaukee, Wisconsin 53202

Philadelphia Museum of Art
Philadelphia, Pennsylvania 19101

Shaker Historical Society Museum
Shaker Heights, Ohio 44120

Shaker Museum
Old Chatham, New York 12136

Shaker Museum
Sabbathday Lake Shaker Community
Poland Spring, Maine 04274

Shaker Village, Inc.
East Canterbury, New Hampshire 03224

Shakertown at Pleasant Hill, Inc.
Harrodsburg, Kentucky 40330

Shakertown at South Union
South Union, Kentucky 42283

Shelburne Museum
Shelburne, Vermont 05482

Smithsonian Institution
Washington, D.C. 20560

Western Reserve Historical Society
History Museum
Cleveland, Ohio 44106

BOOKS
Andrews, Edward D., *The Community Industries of the Shakers.* Emporium Publications, 1971.

Andrews, Edward Deming and Faith:
Religion in Wood. Indiana University Press, 1966.
Shaker Furniture. Dover Publications, Inc., 1964.

Klamkin, Marion, *Hands to Work.* Dodd, Mead & Co., 1972.

Meader, Robert F. W., *Illustrated Guide to Shaker Furniture.* Dover Publications, Inc., 1972.

Shea, John G., *The American Shakers and Their Furniture.* Van Nostrand Reinhold Company, 1971.

Sprigg, June, *By Shaker Hands.* Alfred A. Knopf, Inc., 1975.

Shaving Mugs
Objets d'Art from the Barbershop

Men have been shaving for some 4,000 years. But few shaving artifacts have acquired such a determined following of collectors as the personalized shaving mugs that appeared in America after the Civil War, flowered through the Victorian age and vanished—a casualty of World War I—in the early 1920s. No other country had them.

Unpersonalized mugs were, of course, used in many countries over many centuries, and fine old examples are prized antiques. However, the interest of shaving-mug collectors is concentrated on the type that became popular in America in the late 1860s, when beards went

---

Burt Handelsman, a real estate investor in White Plains, New York, got the first of his 500 shaving mugs as a gift from his fiancée, now his wife.

---

out of style. Shaving at home with the old straight razor was difficult, even perilous, and patronage of the barbershop increased. For hygienic reasons, barbers began to provide a mug, suitably identified, for each regular customer, so that the customer's own soap and brush made the necessary lather for his personal use.

Fine shaving mugs, custom-decorated, were popular as gifts. Photographs—of the owner, his family or a favorite painting—were reproduced by using the ceramic as a base for a photographic emulsion, then burning in the resulting image in a kiln. On simpler mugs the customer's name was added to a stock floral design. More elaborate (and valued) examples have patriotic motifs or designs celebrating fraternal orders or popular sports. But the mugs collectors seek most have a special type of decoration: designs or scenes that indicate the occupations of the mugs' owners. This category—"occupationals"—is the core of any serious collection. In my collection, I can contemplate John C. Hendrix, portrayed on a mug addressing a jury in his role as attorney *(page 150)*.

My Mr. Hendrix is special because lawyers, doctors and other professional men were less inclined to advertise themselves, even within the clubhouse atmosphere of the barbershop, than were the more gregarious merchants and tradesmen of the neighborhood. A professional man's shaving mug, therefore, is less likely to surface and is worth more when it does. A doctor's mug is

particularly desirable. It may suggest his profession with a skull and crossbones; more common and less macabre is a horse and buggy to symbolize night house calls.

There are some 600 occupations—including barbering—represented in mug collections. Apart from the professions, uncommon occupations, such as deep-sea diver, and those no longer practiced, such as wheelwright, are the hardest to find illustrated, and such mugs command the highest prices. One of the most prized occupationals is the undertaker's—in 1978 one example was reported to have gone at auction in California for $800.

I have a strong attachment to two other occupational mugs in my collection because of the way I acquired them; one is an optician's, the other a stage magician's. The optician's mug I saw in a barbershop in Brooklyn. The shop owner, whom my father knew, was in New Jersey hiding out from the New York police. In his absence, his brother was running the shop, and he refused to sell the mug I coveted. My father arranged for me to pick up the owner on the New York-New Jersey border one morning, an hour after midnight. I drove him to his shop, he opened it and I had my optician's mug.

The magician's mug had belonged to Harry Kellar, a famous stage personality who taught Houdini and others their craft. I saw his mug in a dealer's private collection. It portrayed two little red devils whispering into Kellar's ears. For years I begged to be allowed to buy this gem but the dealer refused to part with it. After seven years I got a call. The dealer was very ill, dying in fact, and wanted to say that he was leaving the mug to me.

Such mugs represented membership in the male club that the barbershop provided for many decades. Each man took pride in his mug, which the barber ordered for him. Many supply companies maintained special departments to satisfy the demand.

The largest company was the Koken Barber Supply Company of St. Louis, which produced as many as 90 hand-painted mugs a day. Other firms whose names collectors might find on the bottom of the mugs include

---

This shaving mug is prized because it has all the desired collectible attributes: the owner's name, an imposing symbol of his occupation as an engineer (a railroad bridge, perhaps one he built), and his photograph.

The unusual silver-plated mug above, labeled "The Utility Shaving Mug," was made for home use. It has a drawer for storing soap and a separate compartment for holding the brush.

This scuttle-shaped mug from about 1890 has a small mirror at the side. The spout allowed water to be poured out after use.

A patented mug has a small compartment for soap, separate from the larger compartment for water. Such unadorned mugs are easy to find.

Smith Brothers of Boston; Theo A. Kochs Company of Chicago; B. Stuebner's Sons of Brooklyn; Lewis Stenger Company of Portland, Oregon; E. Berninghaus of Cincinnati; Hecker Brothers of Kansas City, Missouri; and Hytes Company of Topeka, Kansas.

The mug itself began as pure white pottery, imported ready-made but unadorned from Europe. Many mugs bore marks still recognized today, such as Limoges and Sèvres. Most mugs of American porcelain were considered inferior—the main United States company whose mugs were thought worth personalizing was the Homer Laughlin China Company of East Liverpool, Ohio.

The artists who did the painting and lettering are for the most part anonymous—only occasionally is a signature found, and it usually adds little to the value. However, each year the artists received a bonus that arose from the nature of their work. Real gold was used for lettering and decoration. To recover bits of the precious metal that would otherwise be lost, it was customary once a year to burn the rags the artists used to wipe their brushes. All artists in an establishment shared in the value of the gold recovered from the ashes.

The decline of the shaving mug in the early 20th Century took place almost as rapidly as its popularity had grown in the 1860s. One cause of the decline was the introduction of the safety razor and disposable blade by King Camp Gillette in 1903. By 1906 his company was producing nearly a quarter million razors and over one million blades annually. Personal shaving became even more common after World War I, when servicemen had to shave themselves. Finally, the spread of blue laws forced Sunday closings and lessened the social function of the barbershop, for which the Sunday trade had been important. But by the 1930s, just as dust was beginning to settle on shaving mugs, collectors had already begun to seek out those hidden away in attics or unused back rooms of once-glorious barber emporiums. And they are still at it.

Most concentrate the searching in the major Eastern cities, particularly in New England, and in Missouri, Illinois and Kansas. Look for old barbershops in towns that once were flourishing and are now in decline; some mugs may linger there. You are likely to have little luck in the South or the West except at estate sales.

The Old Mug Reborn

Decorated mugs—some striking reproductions of authentic shaving collectibles—continue to be manufactured to hold coffee, soup, pencils or even shaving soap. Most are imports, identifiable by the name of the country of origin on the bottom.

Decorated shaving mugs have also been put out as part of promotion campaigns. The most notable of these was the series advertising the Sportsman line of men's toiletries. More than 375,000 were issued, all hand-painted but inscribed in a way that would make it impossible to confuse them with collectible mugs from the pre-World War I period.

The name of a vocation (or avocation), rather than the owner's name, was painted on the series issued by the Lambert pharmaceutical company in the 1950s. Collectible shaving mugs show the owner's name.

Razors' Progress: Elegance to Practicality

Although mugs are the most avidly collected shaving equipment, many people also seek old razors. They are remarkable for the variety and ingenuity of their designs and for the workmanship and materials lavished on their manufacture. The straight razor first appeared in Western Europe around 1600, although clean-shaven faces have been the male style at various periods dating back at least to the 12th Dynasty (1991-1786 B.C.) in Egypt. Implements that have been used include sharks' teeth, clamshells, a Bronze Age device shaped like a spoon with a sharp V notch and, the most common, knives.

By the early 1800s fine straight razors (notably from several firms in Sheffield, England, and from the Krupp steel-works in Germany) had attained uniform high quality; manufacturers began to ornament both blades and handles. Many handles were made of silver or gold, decorated with inlay, or hand-carved of ivory, fine wood, bone, tortoise shell, horn or mother-of-pearl.

The straight razor gave way soon after the turn of the century to the Gillette safety razor, which inspired a host of rival types. All—old Gillettes as well as other strange contraptions—are fairly easy to find. Presumably the electric shavers that more recently have challenged blade razors also will become collectibles.

On these 19th Century straight razors the handles are: tortoise shell (top) on the Master razor, made in Connecticut; wood (center), from Sheffield, England; and flower-decorated plastic, from Germany.

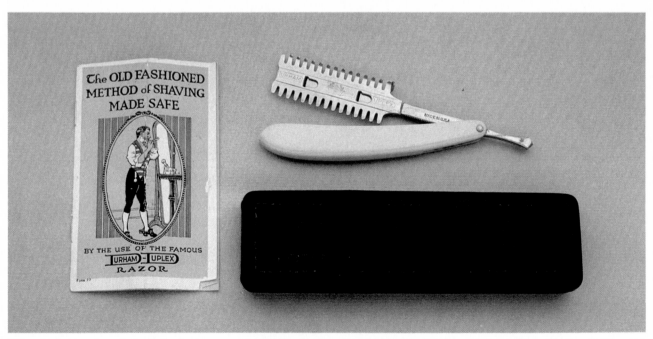

"The old-fashioned method of shaving" was made safe by this Durham-Duplex adaptation of the straight razor. It had a re-placeable blade under the toothed guard bar. This is a 1907 model, but similar razors were produced for nearly half a century.

American soldiers in World War I received Gillette safety razors like the one at right, in Army-style cases that gave the set its name.

An early Schick injector razor is pictured below with a package of World War I blades. The razor stores blades in the handle. The shaving head swivels to a position parallel to the handle so that a press of the lever injects a fresh blade and ejects the old one.

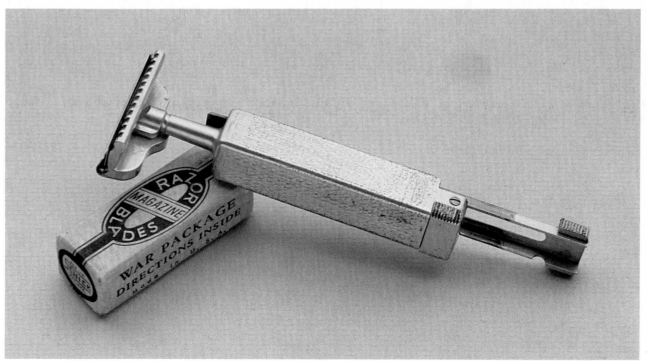

Numbered mugs like this one were kept in hotel barbershops, and were reserved for the use of guests occupying the corresponding room.

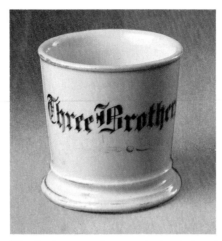

The shaving mug above was probably shared at the barbershop by three brothers. The design is typical of mugs made about 1865.

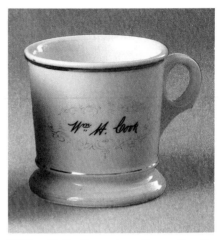

William H. Cook's mug is worth more than the mugs at left because it bears his signature, but is worth less than the ornate ones below.

The elaborate decoration on this mug was probably a stock design that was selected by H. W. Brown from a catalogue.

Paintings, copied photographically onto the ceramic, are a rare decoration, making Edward Meyer's mug valuable.

Flags like the ones on Harry T. Barnett's mug were a fairly common decoration. In some cases, they honored the owner's ancestry.

Typical of the many fraternal mugs is this one, which bears symbols associated with the order of Free and Accepted Masons.

Membership in a Civil War veterans' organization—the G.A.R. had posts numbered 115 in many states—is indicated on this mug.

A sport—as a profession or avocation—was often portrayed on mugs. The bicyclist's mug above is an interesting but not rare example.

R. Arken's name is tucked among symbols of 19th Century America: a locomotive, telegraph lines, the Statue of Liberty, an eagle and a steamship.

Butchers' mugs are fairly common occupationals, and their worth varies according to the detail of the illustration. The examples above increase in value left to

right, from the steer's head, a stock design and the least prized, to the very valuable mug with the detailed scene of a butcher cutting up a carcass at the far right.

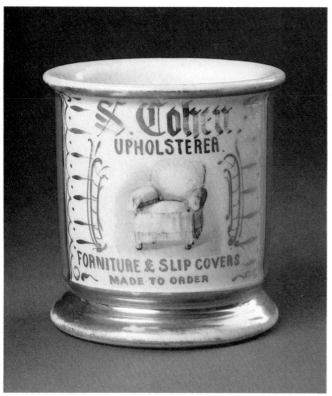

Two factors—a misspelling and a Jewish name, seldom found on collectible shaving mugs—make the mug above distinctive and valuable.

This rare occupational mug—it belonged to a motorized-bus tour guide—is a reminder of the early automotive age.

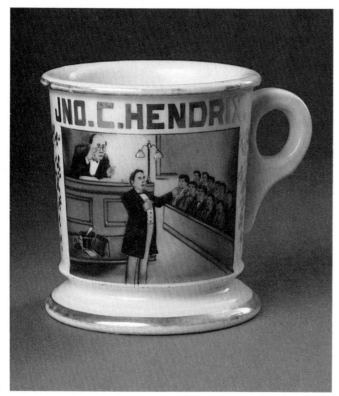

A courtroom scene appears on a mug that belonged to lawyer John C. Hendrix. Few mugs depicting a professional's work are found.

An unusual photographer's mug shows a design—camera and globe—used to indicate an occupational connection with the news world.

Mugs picturing obsolete occupations are highly prized. A tree-stump puller is represented on the mug at the left. In the center, a millstone dresser sharpens a stone for grinding grain. At right, a manure collector waits to clear the tracks after the passage of horse-drawn trolleys.

For his shaving mug the famous stage magician Harry Kellar had himself portrayed with two red devils cavorting on his shoulders.

MUSEUMS
Atwater Kent Museum
Philadelphia, Pennsylvania 19106

Fort Worth Museum of Science and History
Fort Worth, Texas 76107

The Institute of Texas Cultures Museum
University of Texas
San Antonio, Texas 78284

Lightner Museum
St. Augustine, Florida 32084

The New-York Historical Society
New York, New York 10024

BOOKS
Powell, Robert Blake:
Antique Shaving Mugs of the United States. Published by the author, 1333 Kathryn Street, Hurst, Texas 76053, 1972.
Occupational and Fraternal Mugs of the United States, 1978.

Ware, W. Porter, *Price List of Occupational and Society Emblems Shaving Mugs.* Lightner Publishing Corp., 1949.

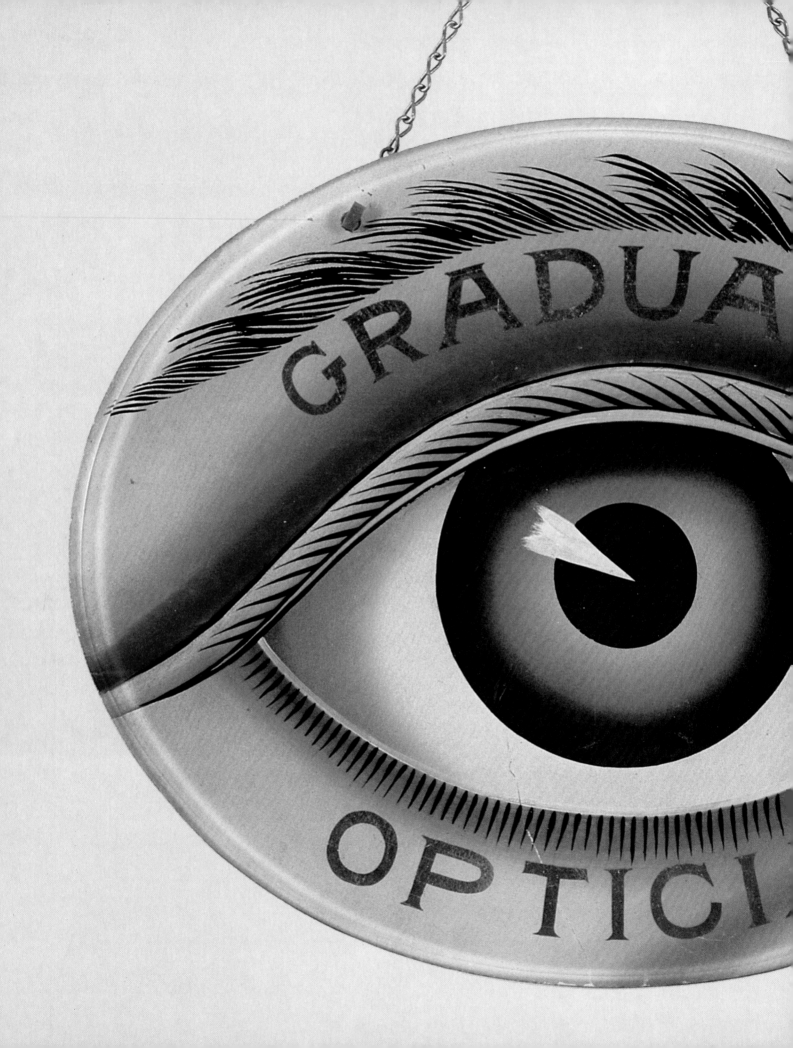

Signs
Eye Catchers
That Inform

One sign collector I know was driving back roads in Maine looking for yard sales when he came upon a sale that he knew had something he wanted even before he stopped his car and got out. He dickered with the homeowner and for six dollars came away with the sign advertising the sale. It was a heavy, round piece of metal on a stand-up post with YARD SALE crudely hand-lettered over a white painted background. At home, paint remover revealed what my friend had suspected. Under the paint was a 1920s porcelain Valvoline gas sign in excellent condition, worth about 10 times what he had paid.

Old signs—the older the better, although relatively recent neon signs have become popular—are increas-

---

Linda Malkin is an interior designer whose signs fill every room of her home. She specializes in large three-dimensional figures.

---

ingly desirable collectibles. They are valuable as documents of social history and as examples of popular art—many are unusual though primitive folk art, but others are sophisticated and beautiful graphic design.

A sign can be any object of almost any material specifically designed to inform (STOP, 42ND STREET, WET PAINT) or to promote (ED'S LUNCHEONETTE, ATWATER KENT RADIOS). Signs can be huge, like the 20-story-high neon signs that soar over casinos in Las Vegas. And they can be as small as postcards. They can be as permanent as the Roman road markers made of stone that still stand in Europe, 2,000 years after they were installed, and as perishable as a piece of cardboard on a wooden stake bearing the word LEMONADE in a child's scrawl.

The most frequently collected types of signs are the ones that identify places of business and those that advertise products. Practicality requires manageable proportions, 10 feet being about the limit. And the most

---

An early-20th Century eye, 18 inches wide, is painted on the back of a piece of glass that once hung in the front window of a shop. It is desirable because it imitates the form of a real object, because its colors are still vivid and because few glass signs have survived.

desirable materials are wood—especially in figures such as the giant three-dimensional shears at right—painted glass, lithographed tin, porcelain and neon. Although paper and cardboard signs also are collected, they are sought mainly by those interested in posters, described in a separate volume of this encyclopedia.

Three-dimensional wooden signs can be very costly because they are desirable as folk art. Tin and porcelain signs can bring anywhere from a few dollars for one that says ROOMS TO LET to more than $1,000 for a lithographed tin sign bearing the Grape Nuts girl and her Saint Bernard, which were once the symbol of the cereal. In any material, prices are highest for signs with pictures—especially of women, children, dogs or products that no longer are sold, such as Richardson's kola gum (Strengthens the weak and quiets the nervous). Especially desired are advertisements for products that were packaged in tins or bottles, because the containers often can be found and displayed with the signs.

The gems among signs, the three-dimensional trade figures that once identified a place of business, are largely gone from the modern landscape. A hundred years ago streets were carnivals of trade figures: The druggist displayed an oversized mortar and pestle, large eyeglasses hung outside the optician's shop, a wooden Indian with cigars in hand identified the tobacconist, a giant molar marked the dentist's location. Today trade figures are found mainly at antique shows and auctions; a sign bearing its maker's signature brings a premium.

Tin and porcelain signs, on the other hand, can sometimes be found where they were first installed. More often they turn up disguised, like my friend's Valvoline sign, or serving an unintended function, such as providing a makeshift floorboard in an old car. Tin signs rust easily but porcelain signs—ceramic-coated steel, as in a bathtub—stand up to weather, even to long burial, if they are not chipped or cracked to expose the metal.

Tin signs were used as early as the beginning of the 19th Century, when they bore painted inscriptions, but it was the perfection of the process of lithographing tin in the 1890s that gave such signs their collectible glory. Tin signs proliferated from the 1890s until World War I, but by the end of World War II they had generally been replaced with plastic. Signs of pre-World War I vintage are the most valuable. A particularly desirable kind is the so-called self-frame sign, which looks like a picture in a frame. Also desirable is the die-cut type, such as the paint sign on page 156, cut in a figure shape. Because lithographed tin signs were expensive, they were often lent by a company rather than simply given to the business where they were displayed. Any sign with a printed statement on the back such as "Property of Buster Brown Company, Please Return" brings a premium. Sign collectors call these self-documented signs.

Wooden shears five feet long, which once hung outside a cutlery shop, are extremely valuable because they were made by a notable carver, Samuel Robb, who worked in New York City in the late 19th Century.

Condition is an important determinant of value in tin signs; they are graded on a scale of 1 for the poorest to 10 for a sign in new condition. A grade 10 sign can be worth 15 to 20 times as much as a similar one of grade 3 or 4. Age can be determined roughly by examining the lithography with a magnifying glass: Signs with a regular pattern of dots were made with a photolithographic process, and date from the time of World War I.

Porcelain signs, such as the Rouses Point Bridge sign on page 159, were made during the same period as tin signs. Porcelain signs resemble tin signs and are valued by the same criteria. Their chief virtues are their glossy finish and durability.

The newest and flashiest collectible signs are neon. They first appeared in the United States in 1924; a Packard dealer brought home two from France, where they were invented, and caused traffic jams in downtown Los Angeles when he turned them on. From California neon swept across the country. The most collectible neon signs are small modern versions of the old trade figures: the outline of a fish from a seafood market, the outline of a shoe from a shoe-repair shop, or an upraised hand from a palm reader's establishment. Beer and automobile-showroom neons are very easy to find.

Expensive to make, neon signs began to be replaced in the 1960s with plastic lighted by fluorescent tubes. But many still exist; if you know of a neon-repair shop, look for signs that are out of order. They can usually be had for almost nothing and can be fixed at modest expense.

For related material, see the articles on Advertising Giveaways, Automobilia and Posters in separate volumes of The Encyclopedia of Collectibles.

Hand-painted on front and back, this wooden watch, two feet in diameter, was created by R. Nadeau, of Rumford, Maine, who put his name and city at the bottom of the dial. Like the other signs on this page, it is valuable folk art.

Inside the late-19th Century copper boot above was a gaslight, its glow visible through perforations outlining the shape and trade name.

A rare double-sided sign, die-cut of tin in the early 20th Century, hung over a hardware-store counter with a pail that contained a ball of string used for tying parcels. The sign is especially valuable because the Dutch boy is still advertising paint.

Likenesses Larger than Life

Display facsimiles, in a sense the descendants of the old three-dimensional trade figures, were set up in stores to advertise products rather than identify a business. They are much easier to find than the trade figures, many of which are preserved in museums.

Facsimiles are larger than the products they imitate and promote, but most are smaller than trade figures—they had to fit on a countertop or hang in the relatively cramped quarters of a shop. Some, such as the tin varnish can pictured at left, are built of the same material as their life-sized cousins. Others, such as the pen below, which is wood and brass, are simply made to resemble the original.

Both age and product recognizability are factors in value; a plastic Heinz salad-dressing bottle standing two feet tall is highly desirable even though it dates only to the 1930s. The Waterman pen is prized both for its workmanship and for its association with the now-defunct pen company.

A real paintbrush lies near a varnish can 30 inches high. The can, which once sat on the counter in a Canadian hardware store, has storage drawers in the back.

A Waterman display pen that hung over a stationery counter in the 1920s is pictured alongside a real bottle of ink to indicate its size; the pen is three feet long.

Listing ticket prices as if they would never change, a valuable porcelain sign from the 1920s specifies bus service between Connecticut towns. It was found bolstering a building in a junkyard.

A simple Massachusetts road sign from the 1920s is two feet high and three inches wide. A porcelainized metal sign like this, with lettering only, is easy to find.

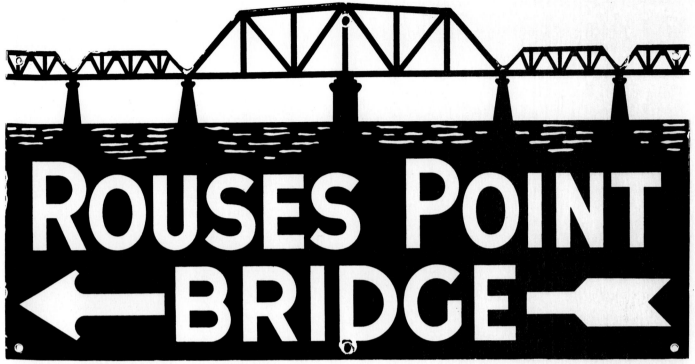

A porcelain directional sign from the New York-Vermont border is desirable because it has a picture and because the maker is identified on the back.

Copying the Immovable

Rubbings enable you to collect the appearance of some signs that cannot be removed, providing a direct copy on paper. The sign must have some relief; that is, the design must be created by a raised surface. The materials needed for making a rubbing are a wide, flat crayon, strong but lightweight paper, scissors for cutting the paper, masking tape for fastening the paper to the sign, and a stiff-bristled brush for cleaning the surface of the sign. The flat edge of the crayon, not the point, is rubbed across the paper to pick up the raised areas of the design.

A rubbing of a familiar movie studio name was taken from a plaque decorating the 4,000-seat theater in the old Paramount Building in New York's Times Square.

A neon sign advertising a luncheonette and the brand of syrups it used in concocting sodas and sundaes dates from the 1950s. The sign is conve- *niently modest in size —two feet across—and has not been made since 1969, two factors that make it highly desirable.*

MUSEUMS
The Museum of Transportation
Boston, Massachusetts 02110

The New-York Historical Society
New York, New York 10024

COLLECTORS ORGANIZATIONS
National Association of Paper & Advertising
Collectors
P.O. Box 471
Columbia, Pennsylvania 17512

Porcelain Advertising Collectors Club
P.O. Box 381
Marshfield Hills, Massachusetts 02051

BOOKS
Fried, Frederick, *Artists in Wood.* Bramhall House, 1970.

Stern, Rudi, *Let There Be Neon.* Harry N. Abrams, Inc., 1979.